TO: JULIE

HAPPY MOTHER'S
DAY!!!

Way Back When:
Santa Barbara in 1914

By Betsy J. Green

Betsy J. Green

MAY 7, 2015

PUBLISHED   November, 2014

PUBLISHER   El Barbareño Publishing, Santa Barbara, CA
www.elbarbareno.com

Printed and bound in the United States

ISBN   978-0-9821636-3-4

PRODUCTION   Design & Layout: Anna Lafferty of Lafferty Design Plus, Santa Barbara, California

ACKNOWLEDGEMENTS   My heartfelt thanks and gratitude for everyone who helped me in my exploration of Santa Barbara's past, especially Neal Graffy, and also Hattie Beresford, Kathi Brewster, Bob Carlson, Marcos Christodoulou, Polly Clement, Darlene Craviotto, Marla Daily, Trish Davis, Dana Driskel, Dave Everett, John Fritsche, Tonia Guerrero, Dona Haber, Anna Lafferty, Joan Easton Lentz, Danielle Levi-Alvares, Milton Love, Lisa Lunsford, Nancy J. McCreary, Dana Newquist, Gail Osherenko, Judy Pearce, Michael Redmon, Cheri Rae, Steve Windhager, John C. Woodward, Michael Ullemeyer, and all the reference librarians at the Santa Barbara Public Library.

WAY BACK WHEN IN SANTA BARBARA

Here are some of the dozens of unsolicited testimonials from the thousands of people who read Betsy's history & humor column on Edhat.com each month.

*(The people posting comments have not received
any compensation such as insider trading tips,
samples of prescription drugs, or "get out of jail free" cards.)*

"Another fun to read history lesson!"

*"Thanks, as always, for another informative
and humorous look at old S.B."*

A LOT OF WORK HERE THAT IS MUCH APPRECIATED! KEEP UP THE GOOD WORK!"

"Very interesting and very amusing. Thanks."

**"GREAT!!!
Thank you Betsy for another wonderful view into the "Good Old Days" of SB.
Interesting and engaging!!!!"**

"Thanks, Betsy for so many interesting facts about Old Santa Barbara."

"Once again, Betsy hits it out of the park!"

"Thank you for this great 'post from the past.'"

But wait, there's more!!!!

"Lovely article. I like your style."

"Oh Betsy! This is great! I'm sharing it with everyone. Thank you for the gift of history."

"Great research and nicely written. Thank you, Betsy."

"Thank you, Betsy, ¡muy divertido y informativo!"

*"Hey, Betsy, I like your story!
    It was very informative and I appreciate the effort you put into it."*

"You do a wonderful job, Betsy, with your history columns."

"Count me as another very appreciative fan."

"Thank you Betsy – always a delightful and informative read!"

"Such fun reading – thank you!"

"Great history with delightful commentary. Thank you!"

*"Very cool article. Thank you for taking the time to put it together and sharing it with us.
    I love your writing style."*

"*As always, I love these posts of Betsy's.*
***Can't wait for the book!*"**

Dedication

This book is dedicated to the editors and writers who worked for the Santa Barbara *Morning Press* and *Daily News & Independent* in 1914 – and preserved the history of everyday life for us to enjoy 100 years later. All quotes in this book are from these two papers, unless otherwise noted.

Way Back When: Santa Barbara in 1914

Tales of everyday life based on articles in the *Morning Press* and *Daily News & Independent* in 1914

The year started off with dirty dancing – the tango! – which critics claimed led to "looseness of morals." Perhaps because our city seemed to be racing down the Road to Perdition (tsk, tsk!), the American Baptist Publication Society parked their chapel car at our train station and attempted to save wayward souls. And maybe it was Divine Justice! that January ended with a horrendous flood. Did we learn our lesson and mend our ways? What do *you* think?

Tidal waves of biblical proportions killed thousands of Californians – according to newspapers in Europe. Imagine that! Newspapers spreading misinformation and false rumors. How about cars attacking people? Now, that *was* a true story. Cranking your car could break your arm – one Santa Barbara man discovered this painful truth. Ye gads! Who *can* we trust? Well, at least we could console our palates with Saratoga chips.

The month started off with a stunt plane spiraling out of control at Hope Ranch as the unsuspecting spectators cheered and applauded. Oops! The unrehearsed landing in the tree was *not* part of the act. The stunt dog diving from 75 feet above State Street *was* part of an act. Robbers wearing shoes 11 inches long and 4 1/2 inches wide used nitroglycerin to blow open the post office safe in Ojai and disappeared with the dough. Clowns behaving badly?

Step right up, ladies and gentlemen! The-one-and-the-only Buffalo Bill Cody! came riding into Santa Barbara with the circus. There were no more hostile Indians left here for him to fight – good thing he brought some along with him. For people who wanted to see more action, the-one-and-the-only Mexican rebel General Pancho Villa! charged across the big screens in movie theaters here. Eat some raisins on National Raisin Day (April 30).

Men were in the news this month – bowling in their underwear, dressing in drag, and wearing Panama hats that didn't really come from Panama. Doing *what* in their underwear? Well, you have a look and decide for yourself. A cult group fleeing Los Angeles came to Santa Barbara preaching that the world was coming to an end. Santa Barbarans shrugged their shoulders, said "Meh," and the group moved on in their search for Truth, Beauty, and the Stairway to Heaven.

Sex at the Arlington Hotel, forbidden fruit, and *al fresco* affairs. Nothing was what it seemed to be in Santa Barbara 100 years ago. Is it any better today? Hmmm… Say, did you ever wonder if those knee-length bathing suits took too much water out of the ocean? Should bathers be forced to wring out their suits before stepping onto the sand? And then some guy shot another guy in Austria. Meh!

Santa Barbara celebrated Independence Day with dynamite and gasoline, an X-rated movie, and a movie dog who confused Art and Life. Sounds like some people today. Some Civil War vets bravely marched in the July 4th parade, but the newspaper predicted they wouldn't be around next year. Thanks a lot! Peter-the-movie-dog rescued someone in a scene who was having an Oscar-winning moment and only pretending to be drowning, but must have been doing a darned good job.

Well, the Old Spanish Days were *pasado*, and [spoiler alert!] Fiesta was still 10 years away, so what did we do in Santa Barbara in August in 1914? We went to Stearns Wharf and looked at bags of walnuts, watched glowing fish slithering in the slimy sea at night, and some of us wore other people's swimsuits. Eww! But *la crème de la crème* of Santa Barbara headed uptown to the new El Mirasol Hotel.

A couple of unusual characters visited our fair city this month. How unusual? After being visited by Buffalo Bill and his Indians, a group of wackos escaping from Armageddon, and guy named Sex, how does one define unusual? Well, Santa Barbarans just *know*, that's all. Anyway, now that we've settled that, I can tell you that Mule Man and Rattlesnake Jim graced our fair city with their presences in September. And hardly a month went by that there wasn't a story about someone using an explosive substance – for good or for evil.

Santa Barbara High School graduate Martha Graham danced her way out of Santa Barbara and onto stages all over the world. Electric cars hummed their way around the town and into the movies. A cow took a tour of State Street one night, and a dog rode on a streetcar. Which one was smarter? And whiskey made a positive contribution to the health of citizens here.

Just in time for Thanksgiving, kitchen cabinets and slow cookers arrived in Santa Barbara. Or you could have turkey dinner with all the trimmings for $1. A new building appeared in the Funk Zone and is still here today. A Santa Barbara ship captain had a close encounter with a German warship in the Channel.

Christmas 1914 style meant toys under the tree, electric lights on the tree, and Santa Barbara's community tree lighting – but not the tree you're thinking of! Charlie Chaplin was a hit in the theaters. Roses from Santa Barbara were shipped to Pasadena (didn't they have enough of their own?) for the Rose Parade, and a star fell on Mission Canyon – or did it?

> *"All I know is what I read in the papers."*
>
> – Will Rogers, c. 1915

On New Year's Eve in Santa Barbara, as partygoers bid adieu to 1913, a controversial dance appeared on the scene here as it did all over the world.

Image: courtesy of the State Library of New South Wales

Dirty Dancing

"No social season is complete without a fad, and this year the fad is the tango," gushed one society columnist in the local paper. The tango was clearly the hot dance a century ago.

"What do you mean *was*?" asked Marcos Christodoulou, a local booster of the tango.

"On New Year's Eve this year, as on every other one in recent memory, Santa Barbara tango aficionados danced the year away in high heels, warm embraces, and dreamy trances.

"This dance, it turns out, which had its golden age almost a century ago, is alive and well in Santa Barbara and practically every other community on every continent of this otherwise unromantic world.

"Nearly 100 strong (if you count their fanatic brethren in the corridor that runs from San Luis Obispo to Ventura), they have several opportunities to dance weekly, both less formally during weeknight get-togethers, and in larger, dressier events on weekends."

Tango Warnings – "Looseness of Morals"!

Not everyone was taking to the tango back in 1914. In Rome, the pope declared that the tango "outrages modesty," and added, "The people must be made to see the grave offense to God and the irreparable harm to society by participating in spectacles which incite looseness of morals." If that weren't enough to make you sit out this fad, the *Journal of the American Medical Association* declared that "elderly [tango] dancers were in danger of putting too great a strain on a dilated heart or an arteriosclerotic artery."

While some people celebrated the New Year by dancing the tango, others celebrated by taking to the trails.

Image: courtesy of Nancy J. McCreary whose grandparents appear in the photo of La Cumbre Rock.

◇◇◇◇◇◇◇◇◇◇◇◇◇◇◇◇

Anything Goes!

First the tango, then a glimpse of stocking. What next? An article about Paris fashions opined, *"Instead of being discreetly draped, the ankles will now be freely displayed."*

(What would they say if they knew of all the other body parts that would be freely displayed 100 years later?)

A Peak Experience

1914 was the year that hiking earned its place as a fashionable activity in Santa Barbara. This new surge in hiking's popularity originated with a group known as "The Hikers" who almost single-handedly propelled the sport to new heights. I talked to Dave Everett, author of the forthcoming book *Rediscovering the Trails of Mission Canyon.* He told me, "La Cumbre, above all others, was the peak which all trail users aspired to ascend. Atop this peak stood a large rock, referred to then as 'La Cumbre Rock,' which graced many a hiker's photograph (see left). This rock became synonymous with the peak itself and would be immortalized over the years with a 30-foot flagpole placed in a ceremony in 1904, and a Masonic Square and Compass carved into the rock during another ceremony in 1909."

"Good luck finding this rock today," continued Everett. "Most of the top of La Cumbre Rock was blasted away in 1923 when forest rangers used it as the foundation for the city's first fire lookout, leaving only a survey marker and the flagpole intact. The remainder of this rock, however, can still be found behind a communication building and chain-link fence, standing guard over the city and pocked with plenty of reminders of its colorful past."

Most of La Cumbre Rock was blasted out of existence in 1923, according to author Dave Everett.

Image: Dave Everett

No Affluenza Defense

Two "juvenile burglars" who broke into a home in Goleta and stole jewelry, clothes, and blank checks were apprehended and taken to court. Since they had prior offenses, both youngsters were given five-year sentences — one in Folsom Prison and the other in San Quentin State Prison! The local newspaper applauded the judge who, it said, "served notice on other would-be criminals throughout the state that the man who breaks the law in Santa Barbara County will henceforth be made to bear the punishment."

CRIME REPORT

Drug Smuggling Then & Now

Today it's Mexican *panga* boats smuggling bales of marijuana onto our shores. Back in 1914, it was Chinese guys smuggling cans of opium. An immigration officer from Santa Barbara was part of a team of officials who captured a 70-foot-long powerboat carrying 16 illegal immigrants from China and 175 cans of opium. The boat was spotted in the Santa Barbara Channel and later apprehended in Monterey Bay.

Summerland Man Was #1

Unfortunately, this was not an honorable spot to be in. On New Year's Day in 1914, a Summerland driver was one of the first in the state to be arrested for drunk driving, under the new law that made it a misdemeanor for any person to drive an automobile while intoxicated. The man and three companions, in the early morning hours, passed another car near what is now the Andree Clark Bird Refuge, and managed to end up in the drink (pun intended!). The police arrived and determined that the driver was drunk. He was denied bail until he sobered up. No Breathalyzer tests back then!

Alley Oops!

Drinking alcohol just wasn't as much fun in 1914 as it had been in 1913. Two new laws went into effect in January and tripped up a number of local tipplers. In downtown Santa Barbara, starting on January 9, swilling alcoholic beverages on the streets and alleys was no longer permitted. One paper wrote, "If the boys want to take a little sociable nip together, they'll have to hire a hall or find some secluded place, where policemen never trod. Up to this time, they have used the alleys."

Apparently, some saloons in town used to sell booze at the back door for those who preferred to drink their alcohol *al fresco*. Perpetrators were fined $10 to $100, or sentenced to one to 10 days in jail. A beer distributor, possibly alarmed at how this new legislation could give alcohol a bad name, ran an ad in a local paper for Rainier Beer that advised,

"Don't shy at beer as a beverage because some people misuse it. There is more genuine merit as a tonic, as a blood maker in a good beer than you may have supposed. One trial of a good beer will convince you."

The beer distributor here may have been getting nervous about Californians voting for prohibition in November 1914.

FASHIONS

The bird feathers, no doubt, contributed to the "niftiness" of the hats.
Image: *Morning Press*, January 4, 1914

"Nifty Spring Hats"

The fashion for feathers continued in spite of 1913 legislation that prohibited the spring hunting and marketing of migratory birds and the importation of wild bird feathers.

Gail Osherenko, who has taught environmental law and policy at UCSB and is on the Board of the Environmental Defense Center, told me, "Certainly the 1913 law and the International Migratory Bird Treaty [of 1918] were early steps of a fledgling conservation movement. … The 1913 treaty was an important early conservation agreement and fundamental to intervention of the federal government in wildlife law which up until then was the purview of states and not the federal government."

Ooh! La! La! 1914 was the Year of the Ankle.
Image: *Morning Press,* 1914

◇◇◇◇◇◇◇◇◇◇◇◇◇◇◇◇

Image: *Daily News & Independent,* January 23, 1914

Déjà Vu All Over Again?

This photo may surprise the youth of 2014 who think they are being *au courant* by wearing their hats backward. (Good taste never goes out of style, eh?) Beachey was an aviation superstar until his death in 1915.

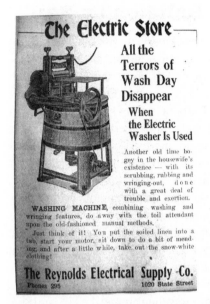

Mondays were hated washdays for many housewives in Santa Barbara.

Image: *Morning Press*, Jan. 18, 1914

Washday Terrors!

The "terrors of wash day?" Really now! Boring, back-breaking, time-consuming drudgery, yes. But terrors? Maybe the ad was referring to mixing water and electricity back in the days before GFCIs (ground fault circuit interrupters). That would scare the heck out of me. Not to mention getting your you-know-what caught in the wringer!

Storm Survivors

January 1914 began with a tango and ended with a torrent that people talked about for decades. Sunday afternoon and evening, January 25, the skies opened up and deluged our city with 9.41 inches of rain. "Houses Carried Away; Bridges Torn Out; Boulevards Wrecked. … Three bridges along Mission Creek were carried out by the flood and two bridges on the east side were destroyed. A number of houses along the creek were also floated away." Ocean waves swept over what is now Cabrillo Boulevard and carried away three sections of pavement 75 to 150 feet long. The beach was covered with sodden belongings, furniture, and even wagons that had been swept along by the wall of water that roared down Mission Creek. Witnesses said it sounded like a freight train.

But eventually the weather cleared. People started to clean up the debris, recount their experiences, and even laugh a little. The newspaper lauded the "telephone girls" — young women who worked the switchboards. "A few words of praise may be given to the 30 … telephone operators … who worked incessantly for hours, answering calls. Many of these girls, without hesitation, left their homes that were being flooded and worked until the rush was over … They did not take time to sit, but stood at the switchboard throughout the long and tedious grind."

image: courtesy of Neal Graffy

A Storm to Remember

Ever ready to take advantage of some free special effects, the folks at the Flying "A" Film Company hastily penned a script that featured a flood. In Oak Park, a cottonwood tree had fallen across the creek, and the movie's heroine was filmed making her way across it, being chased by (who else?) a dastardly villain.

Other residents thought that the flooding was just "ducky." A man who raised chickens and ducks on Pueblo Street near Mission Creek lost many of his cluckers, but not his web-footed fowl. The morning after the flood, he discovered a passel of mud-spattered paddlers looking like they had thoroughly enjoyed themselves. And when workers were moving a house that had floated off its foundation near Bath and Ortega streets, they looked in the flooded foundation and saw "two handsome specimens of mountain trout, measuring seven and eight inches long."

An Edhat reader wrote: My mom was two in 1914, gives me an idea of what was happening. Grandma told me about the 1914 flood, washed lots of top soil onto our property (where mom and later, my brother and I, grew up). A Montecito couple was at a meeting at the Miramar Hotel (our neighbor); they called home to check on the children (left with a nanny). With no answer they worried and decided to go home. Others at the hotel begged them to stay but off they went; their carriage was swept down a creek, both drowned; they were found clinging to each other. The last of their four children died in the last year or so.

The 1914 flood story reminded another Edhat reader about a flood c. 1950: My father had picked me up early from school at La Cumbre knowing that I'd have a hard time riding my bicycle home in the rain and flooding. He took me to Oak Park to watch the water go over the bridge there and then we went to the cafe to get some lunch as the owner was still cooking with his shoes off and pants legs rolled up to near his knees.

And another reader noted that the storm had some benefits: My Grandma said the rich top soil on our family property washed in during the flood.

Religion by Rail

The American Baptist Publication Society apparently decided that if people wouldn't go to church, the church would go to them. On January 4, Santa Barbara was visited by a Baptist "chapel car." (Perhaps the Baptists were hoping to save the souls of local citizens who were tangoing their way to hell.)

A local paper announced that "a special service will be held in the chapel car located just west of the depot, … Chapel car evangelism is a distinctly Baptist enterprise." According to the article, these chapel cars began traveling around the U.S. in 1893.

Words to Live By

It's never too late to make a New Year's resolution. (Hey, it's still January!) So here's one that was in our paper 100 years ago this month, and is still a good way to start the year —

"To live each day as seems best to us, and be tolerant of those who live their own days in their own best way."

This was what happened here, according to Belgian newspapers reporting about January's flood.

Image: detail of Hokusai painting

Tidal Wave Kills 10,000 in California!

Several European papers reported that everywhere from San Jose to Los Angeles was underwater and 10,000 people had been swept away by a tidal wave. Santa Barbara residents received R U OK? telegrams from friends and relatives in Europe.

The newspaper reports went on to say that everyone living inland of a light blue line painted on the streets was spared. (Okay, just kidding about that one!) The exaggerated reports in European newspapers should remind us that just because it's in print (or on the Internet), doesn't mean it's true. As they say in journalism — If your mother says she loves you; check it out! Read more about the flood in the January chapter.

STORM REPORT

Snakes Alive!

A man picking up waterlogged lumber on his property on West Islay Street uncovered a four-foot-long rattlesnake. Two more rattlers were found in the debris piled upstream of one of the bridges over Mission Creek. All three critters were killed.

It's Mine Now

The same January rainstorm (9.41 inches) caused some streams here to change their course. This created problems for landowners whose property descriptions contained the phrase, "to the middle of the creek."

One landowner found herself "in possession of two or three acres which before were on the other side of the creek, upon which are a number of valuable trees. The expense of turning the stream back into its old channel would be greater than the value of the land, so the question is, to whom does the runaway property belong?"

Mission Creek's flooding lifted several houses off their foundations and piled them up at the Haley Street Bridge.

Image: courtesy of Neal Graffy

Oh, Lucky Man!

Franklin Pierce Montgomery was working on a house at Cota and Bath streets and must have had his guardian angel with him this day. As the house was being raised up off its foundation (it was probably displaced by the January flood), it slipped and fell on him.

Fortunately, he had better luck than the Wicked Witch of the East. The soil underneath him gave way and he was not seriously injured, according to the newspaper. I checked the cemetery records here on the Santa Barbara Genealogy Society's website and did not find him buried here, so he must have survived.

Here's One for King Solomon

Another legal question raised by the flooding was, "If a flock of chickens lands in your front yard, through elemental disturbance, to whom do the chickens belong?" Some of the chicken receivers downstream who woke up after the rainstorm and found themselves in possession of a gaggle of cluckers, felt they were entitled to keep the birds.

However, the original chicken owners upstream cried — of course — "Fowl!" Continued the local paper, "There is a crying need of the standardization of the regulations governing ownership of the flotsam and jetsam of Mission Creek." Hmmm. Should salvage rights apply to chickens?

One Edhat reader quipped:

As times change, many things remain exactly the same.

Kitchen Disasters Repurposed?

One of the menu suggestions in the local paper listed "Dropped Eggs." I guess we've all dropped an egg or two in our culinary escapades, but I'd never thought of serving them up, or mentioning that I scraped them up off the floor and cooked them anyway. But never fear, dear readers! A quick perambulation around the Internet revealed that "dropped eggs" is an old-fashioned term for "poached eggs."

An Edhat reader added: When we drop an egg on the floor in my kitchen, the dog yelps "Score!" and knows he's getting a scrambled egg added to his food dish.

And speaking of historic cuisine, here's a recipe that a Santa Barbara newspaper printed for "Saratoga Chips."

"Peel the potatoes carefully, cut into very thin slices and keep in cold water overnight, drain off the water and rub the potatoes between napkins or towels until thoroughly dry, then throw a handful at a time into a kettle or pan of very hot lard, stirring with a fork so that they may not adhere to the kettle or to each other. As soon as they become light brown and crisp, remove quickly with a skimmer and sprinkle with salt as they are taken up." (Saratoga Chips are now called potato chips.)

Downward Dog

Image: *Morning Press,* February 13, 1914

I thought my "downward dog" was pretty good, but this dog has me beat, that's for sure. A trained animal act packed the Portola Theatre in February 1914 to see Teddy, the Russian wolfhound do his thing. He was accompanied by a group of trained goats in tights. (Just kidding about the tights, but there was a trained goat act that warmed up the crowd for the Tedster.)

And by the way — *Teddy,* the Russian wolfhound? Couldn't they come up with a more Slavic-sounding name? How about Vladimir or Yakov or Borat instead?

Here in Santa Barbara, dairy owners on the Mesa ran ads in the paper assuring citizens that they were selling the real deal.

Image: *Daily News & Independent,* February 16, 1914

"Pale Blue Poison!"

People who paid attention in high school English class might recognize this description of adulterated milk from *The Jungle,* Upton Sinclair's 1906 exposé of the unappetizing and dangerous practices in the food industry. The Pure Food and Drugs Act was passed in 1906, but people were still concerned about what was really in what they were eating and drinking.

Car Cranks

Image: courtesy of the New York Public Library

Herbert Earlscliffe of Montecito was cranking the starter on his car when something went horribly wrong and he ended up with a broken arm. Dana Newquist, local classic car collector, told me, "Most cars into the mid 30s had 'crank holes' at the base of the radiator shell for insertion of the crank. … The danger of the crank happens when a person is turning the engine over using the crank and the car 'backfires.' A backfire forces the engine to abruptly reverse direction. If your arm is turning the crank in a clockwise direction when a backfire occurs, the result is often a broken arm." Ouch!

If only Herbert had waited a year! In 1915, a Dayton, Ohio man named Charles Kettering received a patent for the electrical starter motor. He went on to become the founder of Delco. The name Delco comes from Dayton Engineering Laboratories Company.

An Edhat reader added: The impetus for the invention of the electric self-starter was not only broken arms, but forgetting to take your car out of gear, and being run over when your car started! This hurt and killed a number of people, including a close friend of Henry Leland, the owner of Cadillac Motor Car Company. He contacted Charles Kettering, owner of Delco, and in 1911, Kettering devised an electric starter, based on his invention of the electric cash register for NCR. The electric starter, and electric lights first appeared as standard equipment on the 1912 Cadillac, the first car so equipped. For this, Cadillac was awarded the famed Dewar Trophy, given only once a year to a company for excellence in engineering

Image: *Morning Press,* 1914

Ford Tires and Baby's Teeth

This headline caught my eye, and also inspired the witty reply of a newspaper writer. The origin of the remark began with a humorous article in *Harper's Weekly* magazine about the popularity of Ford cars. The writer quipped, "Every second baby you meet is cutting its teeth on a Ford tire."

The newspaper's "Bureau of Superfluous and Erroneous Statistics" replied tongue-in-cheek (pun intended!) that it "has microscopically examined 148,762 Ford tires for infantile teeth marks. It is manifestly difficult with our present equipment to differentiate with scientific accuracy between nail marks, spike marks, tack marks, and infantile teeth marks. … if this investigation is still further to be prosecuted and the teeth-cutting resiliency and prophylactic properties of the Ford tire are to be considered an asset, we recommend the addition of a well-equipped dentist to the staff of this bureau." I couldn't have said it better myself.

A $15,000 House

Well, I never know where a story will take me once I start to dig into it. In this case, an article about a building permit for a home that was estimated to cost $15,000 caught my eye. In 1914, when the average wage earner was taking home $1,266 a year, this was clearly not your average abode. A woman named Miriam R. Vaughan applied for the permit. A little research in the Santa Barbara Public Library and online uncovered the fact that she was the wife of the artist Reginald Wilmer Vaughan, and the mother of their son Samuel Edson Vaughan, also an artist. The Vaughan family lived in their Mediterranean-style home at 316 E. Los Olivos Street until the late 1950s. (The house is still here, and is a City Designated Landmark. Please do not bother the current occupants.)

Reginald studied with Santa Barbara artist Ed Borein, and his son studied with Carl Oscar Borg, another prominent local artist. Some of Reginald's sketches appeared in an exhibit at the Santa Barbara Historical Museum in 2014.

Reginald's son Samuel Edson Vaughan painted one of the WPA murals located in the foyer of the Veteran's Memorial Building at 112 W. Cabrillo Blvd. (This mural, which depicts Europe after World War I, is located up near the ceiling. I almost walked out without seeing it! The mural on the opposite wall was done by another Santa Barbara artist – Joseph Knowles.)

An Edhat reader with a connection to the Vaughan home added this: My family has lived in the aforementioned house since the Vaughans sold it, but I did not know the son painted also. I do know Samuel's daughter and grandchildren and will send this on to them. The house remains essentially unchanged architecturally from when the Vaughans lived here.

WAY BACK WHEN IN SANTA BARBARA

This could be the last photo of the ill-fated plane with the Beachster on the right and Glen Martin on the left at Hope Ranch just before the unhappy landing.   Image: courtesy of Neal Graffy

A rare photo of the daredevil doggie named Queen who wowed 'em on State Street.

Image: *Morning Press,* February 13, 1914

Pilot Cheats Death in Hope Ranch

March 1914 started off with a bang for two high-flying celebrities. Lincoln Beachey, the famous pilot — he who wore his hat backwards — aimed high in the sky over Hope Ranch on March 1. Some 5,000 Santa Barbarans assembled to watch his attempt at a new record for the number of loop-the-loops. (In aviation as with roller coasters, a loop-the-loop is a vertical loop.) After Beachey's first loop at 1,800 feet, he lost control of the aircraft, made 14! unplanned loops, and ended up spiraling to earth and landing in a tree.

Miraculously, Beachey survived with only a scratch on his nose. (As any pilot will tell you – a good landing is one you can walk away from; a great landing is when you can reuse the aircraft.) So, this was a good, but not a great, landing. The plane was totaled, and Beachey himself was so totally disgusted that he said a **bad word** (which the newspapers refused to print) and declared he was done with flying: "My d——d luck! Never again for me!"

Most of the spectators thought it was all part of the act and applauded heartily. Nobody asked for a refund. Even the experts were fooled. "Glen Martin, the aviator, was enthusiastically counting the number of loops and shouted excitedly that Beachey had broken his record by making 14 loops." (Martin was also a pilot and had his own airplane manufacturing company. It survives today as Lockheed-Martin. He is pictured in the photo with Beachey.)

But after a hearty dinner, Beachey calmed down. He made light of his brush with death and his vow to stop flying. Sadly, his luck only lasted for another year. On March 14, 1915, exactly 54 weeks later, Beachey died in San Francisco when his plane broke apart in the air as he was doing loop-the-loops over the bay.

High Diving Act on State Street

Another aerial act in Santa Barbara had a happier outcome a few weeks after the Hope Ranch debacle. A 75-foot ladder was erected on State Street in front of the Mission Theatre (now the Metro 4) and a net was placed below. At 6:45 p.m., the performer simply known as Queen, clad in nothing more than some skimpy black leather straps with large metal studs, climbed the ladder and dove, more or less gracefully, to land safely in the net.

Helen Keller and Anne Sullivan paid a visit to Santa Barbara on their West Coast lecture tour.

Image: courtesy of the Library of Congress

Helen Keller arrived here in March 1914, accompanied by her teacher Anne Sullivan. The two gave a lecture at the Potter Theatre at the corner of State and Montecito streets. The two ladies were giving presentations at numerous other cities at this time, but their stop in Santa Barbara was special because Keller had relatives here. During her brief stopover, she visited her cousins Mary V. and Sally C. Newsum who lived at 1234 Anacapa Street. (I checked. The home is no longer there.)

Celebrity Appearances in Santa Barbara

An Edhat reader wrote this note about the Potter Theatre: My father took part in amateur theatrics there after 1921, when the hotel burned. The theater was a victim of the 1925 earthquake.

Booker T. Washington packed the house at the Normal College on the Riviera.

Image: courtesy of the Library of Congress

The African-American educator, Booker T. Washington spoke at the Normal College on the Riviera where 1500 persons gathered in the courtyard of the school to hear him. Washington was the founder and president of Tuskegee Institute (now Tuskegee University) in Alabama.

Scottish comedian Harry Lauder wowed a local audience during a quick stopover at the Santa Barbara train station.

Image: courtesy of the *New York Evening Journal*

Santa Barbara's train station was the site for a brief but entertaining visit from world-famous vaudeville comedian Scotsman Harry Lauder. He was known for wearing a kilt and carrying a gnarled walking stick. The entertainer gave a brief performance for some 70 Santa Barbarans. "Accompanied by two of his pipers in kilties and full Scotch costume, he gave a short entertainment on the depot platform and was vociferously applauded by his local admirers. He was on his way in his private car from Los Angeles to San Francisco."

No doubt, Lauder had the crowd doubled over with his jokes that usually began, "Hae ye heard this one?" Many of his jokes dealt with the stereotype of penny-pinching Scotsmen, such as: When Hamish discovered a fly in his whiskey; he squeezed the fly before he threw it out.

The First Look You Get at the New Hart Schaffner & Marx Suits for Spring

Image: *Morning Press,* March 13, 1914

The Age of the Auto

The auto era officially rolled onto State Street in March of 1914. "Hitching posts along State Street must go," announced the *Daily News and Independent.* "This morning, the street department started a crew to work on either side of the street digging the posts out of their concrete foundations ... posts which have been doing duty for numerous years have disappeared."

Another sign of "progress" was paved streets. Already in 1914, there were 10 miles of paved streets out of the 80.7 total miles of streets in Santa Barbara. Heavens to Betsy! What's next? Bulb-outs?

Speaking of Scotland, where the game of golf originated, take a gander at what the well-dressed golfer of 1914 was wearing when he played the links at our local courses. Ever wonder how a "sports jacket" got its name? Now you know.

Flattery Will Get You – Arrested

The "right to remain silent" rule had not yet been instituted in law enforcement, and the expression "zip your lip" did not exist in 1914 either since zippers had not been invented yet. Nonetheless, one Santa Barbara resident should have put his brain in gear before opening his mouth to the local police chief. The resident, Charles Berkman, was accused of assaulting another man named Sam Smit. Both were junk dealers. According to the paper, "Berkman fell victim to a little flattery used by the chief in serving the warrant and admitted his guilt." The chief told Berkman that his junk shop was cleaner than Smit's.

"At the mention of his rival's name, Berkman beamed all over. 'Say, chief, I whaled the everlasting stuffing out of that guy yesterday,' chortled Berkman. 'Is that so,' said Chief Ross. 'Well, I've got a warrant for you for battery.'" Berkman was given an "invitation" to explain his actions before a judge.

Sound Causes Silence

The talk of the town in March 1914 was about the first "talking pictures" to be shown in Santa Barbara at the Potter Theatre. The newspaper ads called it "the sensation of the century," and for once this was not empty hyperbole. "The great crowd sat in absolute silence," the *Morning Press* wrote, "as they saw the pictures flashed upon the screen and heard the voice of each character with as much clearness as if the players on the screen were actually talking. ... Without a doubt, these pictures are the best and most entertaining ever presented. There is no doubt the 'talking movies' have come to stay ... "

The inventor of "talking pictures," Thomas Edison, saw pictures with sound as a way of bringing culture to the masses. "The workers deserve and must have more amusement than the richer folk, who are able to afford the regular theater and other expensive pleasures."

Thomas A. Edison c. 1914.

Image: courtesy of the Library of Congress

Tin Can Shack Shelters Hikers

Many of you have probably hiked up Rattlesnake Canyon to Tin Can Meadow and rested before heading back down the trail or heading on up. Back in 1914, the tin can shack was still standing and provided some much appreciated shelter for the hiker's group in a March rainstorm; especially so because it was the first time women were invited to participate in a hike. The group huddled in the shack and built a fire, but after three hours, the deluge continued and the group decided to hike back in the rain. "The walk back was made through the mud, and the girls are deserving of special commendation for the good-natured manner in which they endured the little hardships," wrote the local paper.

"The tin can shack is an odd structure," continued the paper, "erected several years ago by a McConnell, who decided to live in the mountains. He chose this open space at the head of Rattlesnake, but being short of means, gathered all sorts of tin cans in the city. The cans were cut open and the flat tin nailed to a crude framework. The shack is rather picturesque and is of two rooms. It has been abandoned for a long time."

When did the tin can shack pass into history? I asked trail historian Dave Everett, author of the forthcoming book *Rediscovering the Trails of Mission Canyon*. Everett said, "*The Morning Press* in 1918 reported that the roof had caved in and it was starting to fall apart. By 1923, the 'shack' was a pile of tin and wood … The cause of the final destruction was ... weather and 'a group of wayward boys' that finally leveled the building to the ground. … There is no marker of its exact location in the meadow but from photographs I have seen, it was in the upper half of the meadow." Everett also mentioned that the correct name of the shack's builder was William O'Connell.

Santa Barbara historian and Edhat reader Neal Graffy told me that the Flying "A" Film Studio made a movie called The Tin Can Shack.

For the Birds

Bird lovers flocked to the Potter Theatre to see the first Santa Barbara appearance of "the bird man," William Leon Dawson. During his two-hour lecture, Dawson shared his enthusiasm for his feathered friends to the extent that the local paper wrote, "… one doesn't have to go on a far flight of imagination to fancy him a large specimen of long-legged shorebird. I should think his family would live in constant dread lest some fine day, he spread an invisible pair of wings, and soar away back to the wild."

Joan Easton Lentz, author of several bird books and the recent *A Naturalist's Guide to the Santa Barbara Region*, is a great admirer of Dawson and his contribution to birding here. She told me, "Dawson was probably the first ornithologist IN THE WEST to describe birds in a way that would enchant readers, whether they liked birds or not! And he was an ornithologist, and he was the first director of the Santa Barbara Museum of Natural History. Pretty impressive stuff!!"

Dawson's studio in Mission Canyon was named Los Colibris, *which means hummingbirds in Spanish.*
Image: *The Birds of California*

'Tis the Season

Easter fell on April 12 back in 1914. Then, as now, 'twas the season for a religious movie. In 2014, it was Russell Crowe in *Noah*. In 1914, the Palace Theater (motto: "The House of Wholesome Films") was showing a one-reeler called *The Coming of the Padres* produced by the local Flying "A" film studio. This family feature had to compete with a host of other films in Santa Barbara with such titillating titles as *The Girl Who Dared, His Favorite Pastime*, and *Cruel, Cruel Love*.

What does she dare to do? To leave her dysfunctional family behind her!

Image: courtesy of Neal Graffy

Now that the Flying "A" film company had established itself here on Mission Street between State and Chapala streets, other motion picture concerns started to focus on our fair city. The Major Film Manufacturing Company bought several acres on the west side of Santa Barbara between Carrillo and Cañon Perdido streets. And the Diamond Film Company was also looking for property in our area.

I had never heard of these other companies, so I asked Santa Barbara historian Neal Graffy about it. "Everyone seemed to be in a rush to have a studio in Santa Barbara," he said. "The Diamond Film Company leased property on Ortega … The Santa Barbara Motion Picture Co had their studio at 1425 Chapala. … They made at least a half-dozen films." Dana Driskel, studio professor of Film & Media Studies at UCSB, added that one of the films of this last company was recently discovered in New Zealand.

Troop Trains Pass Through Town

Trains full of American GIs trundled through Santa Barbara on their way to Mexico. Am I the only doofus who was unaware that the United States very nearly declared war on Mexico in 1914? Maybe you California-bred folks learned about this in fourth grade. (BTW, dear readers, I'll have you know that I was actually born in California. But I was kidnapped as an infant, and raised by a pack of wolves in New Jersey, and it just took a while for my homing instincts to kick in, that's all. And, no, I can't prove any of this. But on nights when the moon is full, I get this urge to … Oh, never mind.)

Our local newspapers carried headlines such as: "Army Regulars Pass Through on Way to Mexico," and "More Soldiers Pass Through on Way to Border." When two warships cruised down the channel at top speed, scores of enthusiastic Santa Barbarans flocked to the wharf, and "the air echoed with cheers as some of the throngs were carried away with patriotism." Even songwriter Irving Berlin jumped on the bandwagon and wrote *They're on Their Way to Mexico*.

Pancho Villa played himself in what was one of the earliest wars to be recorded on film.

Image: courtesy of the Library of Congress

"The Revolution Will Not Be Televised"

This was according to a beat poet in 1970, but the Mexican Revolution *was* shown on the big screen over at the Mission Theater in 1914, where the main feature was billed as "Mexican War Pictures … Actual photographs of the present war, the pictures taken on the battle line. Biggest and best pictures ever shown of the great Mexican rebellion."

The Mexican general Pancho Villa had signed a movie contract with the Mutual Film Company in January, 1914, and battle scenes were seen on Main Streets (and State Streets) everywhere in the United States. According to an article in *Smithsonian Magazine*, "the Mexican Revolution was an early example of a 20th-century 'media war:' a conflict in which opposing generals duked it out not only on the battlefield, but also in the newspapers and in cinema 'scenarios.'"

An Edhat reader wrote that Pancho Villa's movie was an inspiration: That film about Pancho Villa is so cool! I watched the whole thing even though I don't speak Spanish. There's lots of English in it too. It sure made me want to finish learning Spanish though, so I can understand more than mil novecientos catorce. [1914]

Cavalry at the Ready!

Quadrupeds, as well as bipeds, were also being whipped into a patriotic frenzy. Sherman H. Stowe, a local horseman, sent a telegram to the White House stating, "We are ready to organize and offer to the service of the United States a regiment of California rangers, mounted and equipped." The Santa Barbara County Clerk drew up a list of 4,758 men able to serve in the military, and the local naval reserves were reported to be "drilling diligently."

Raisin' Hell!

April 30 is National Raisin Day, and has been for at least 100 years. Who knew? (National Raisin Day seems to have started around 1910 in Fresno.) The Arlington Grocery here ran an ad featuring 10 different kinds of raisin cakes, raisin pies, and raisin cookies for sale. (We would have to wait until the 1980s for the California Dancing Raisins to sing, *I Heard It on the Grapevine*.)

image: J. D. Hancock

Four Legs Good

But not if you were a ground squirrel. Mexico was not the only battleground in April 1914.

"Supervisors Start Active Campaign Against Squirrels," ran the headline of an article that discussed waging war in the county to wipe out members of the *Spermophilus beecheyi* battalion. "The board proposes to continue the campaign just as long as a squirrel is seen." Official "Squirrel Inspectors" combed the county searching for bipeds harboring enemy squirrels. (Extermination campaigns such as these are why we have driven the ground squirrels to near extinction. Whoops! It's bees, not squirrels, that are disappearing.)

An Edhat reader made a connection between squirrels and Buffalo Bill Cody: As a great (x4) niece of Buffalo Bill Cody, I propose that we reinstate the ground squirrel eradication campaign, and let's add gophers and moles too. In honor of my great (x4) Uncle, I'd like to be able to shoot the little buggers in my own yard. Wait a minute! I promise I'm safe and that no one (other than the rodents themselves) will be harmed by this activity.

Yes, it was the real Buffalo Bill who came to Santa Barbara in April 1914!

Image: courtesy of the Library of Congress

Celebrity Sighting at the Circus

April's visiting celebrity was none other than Buffalo Bill Cody with the circus. The Sells-Floto Circus paraded up State Street with 450 horses, nine bands, lions, and tigers, and bears, oh my! A team of horses stampeded, and as the people stampeded to get out of the way, a woman from Carpinteria was trampled upon and ended up with a broken arm. A good time was had by all. Well, maybe not the lady from Carpinteria.

Twenty-five cents got you into the big tent for the show. And of course Buffalo Bill was the star. One local paper wrote, "To see him ride into the ring, flourish his broad-brimmed Stetson and wave his gray locks is the wild west of song and story incarnated. For a moment, you live in the broad plains, hear the thunder of the hoofs of thousands of buffalo, see the emigrant trains, the soldier camps, and hear the war whoops of the Indians. So long as Buffalo Bill continues to visit us, the romance of the West will live." It's not clear how many more times the famed gentleman made an appearance in Santa Barbara, because the hero of song and story passed into the Great Buffalo Camp in the sky in 1917. (By modern standards, displays of Indians attacking stagecoaches would not be considered politically correct, but at least he used real Indians in his shows.)

Native American Joe Black Fox appeared in Buffalo Bill's shows.

Image: courtesy of the Library of Congress

An Edhat reader was inspired to look for more photos of Joe Black Fox online, and noticed that he "seems quite at ease ...before a camera. Black Fox almost smiles for the portraits. This comfort before the camera was generally uncharacteristic for Native Americans in 1898, for many still believed in the potential for the lens to steal their soul. Black Fox poses first in his feather headdress and then more playfully, with cigarette in hand, relaxed, wrapped in a blanket, and wearing a patterned silken scarf with a pin, earrings, and a beaded lizard-shaped ornament in his hair." He sounds (and looks) like quite a charismatic guy.

But where did they put such a huge assortment of animals and people in Santa Barbara?, I wondered to historian Kathi Brewster. "Much of the lower eastside was similar to the marshy areas near the airport — slough-like," she told me. "The Spanish called it *El Estero*. At one point, there was a track for racing horses, and what we Midwesterners would call a 'Fair or Show grounds.' There was an Agricultural Pavilion where annual exhibitions were held, with tents erected. This would have been south of Haley between Garden, Laguna, and Canal (Olive) Streets, bounded by present day Calle Cesar Chavez. The likely location of a circus."

Adopt-an-Elk?

No, this was not a member of the fraternal organization being discussed in the newspapers here in April 1914.

Miller and Lux, ranchers in Ventura, Kern, and Los Angeles counties apparently had an abundance of the antlered animals and were looking for communities that wanted to foster elk (elks?). Where in Santa Barbara, you ask? There was talk of putting these animals in Oak Park. (Neal Graffy's comment on hearing this – Hey, then they could have called it "Elk Park.")

There were elk on Santa Rosa Island dating back to 1879, according to Marla Daily, president of the Santa Cruz Island Foundation. The majestic herd still existing into the 21st century was slaughtered. She noted, "In my opinion, a poor decision by the Park Service, because they were non-native. Who doesn't love seeing the majestic animals?"

image: Library of Congress

Get Rich Quick c. 1914

I asked Darlene Craviotto, Goleta resident and screenwriter, what she thought about this ad. "I laughed so hard when I read this: 'As it only requires a few hours to construct a complete play, you can readily see the immense possibilities in this work.' And this: 'No literary ability is required, and women have as great an opportunity as men.' Subtext: Because, of course, women have no literary ability at all. I did a quick Google search to find out if it was legit, but I couldn't find any mention of the Photo-Play Association. This looked like a scam — similar to the 'Earn Money at Home' schemes that have been posted throughout the years."

However, Craviotto did some deeper research, and lo and behold, this is what she found in *Women Filmmakers in Early Hollywood* by Karen Ward Mahar: "The early, smaller films (under 1000 ft.) began with impromptu acting (no scripts needed). As films became longer, 'scenarios' became standard and the director-producers wrote their own scenarios. Actors and actresses many times contributed scenarios.

Studios also solicited story ideas from freelance writers, or stole them from other studios and recruited them from contests open to the public. The winners of these contests were frequently female (since they were interested in popular fiction and the movies).

Unsolicited scenarios were accepted by many studios well into the mid 1910s. Contest winners usually made $5 to $15 a scenario — a sum that was considered extremely low (according to *Moving Picture World* in 1910)."

Fingering the Baddies

April 1914 marked the beginning of our local constabulary using fingerprints to help track down criminals. "The local police station is now, for the first time, provided with the finger-marking system with which all the up-to-date police offices of the country are provided, and henceforth it will do its part in assisting in the identification of criminals." I contacted Michael Ullemeyer, Senior Forensic Technician at the Santa Barbara Police Department, to find out when they stopped using ink and paper to make fingerprints. "The Santa Barbara community received an invaluable investigative tool when fingerprints became digitized," he told me. "The Santa Barbara Police Depart

image: Metrónomo

ment installed its first Live Scan fingerprint system back in 1999. We were then able to add to, access and search the growing digital database of known criminal fingerprints both within the State of California and later countrywide via the FBI's IAFIS [Integrated Automated Fingerprint Identification System] ... this technology gave investigators the ability to conduct fast computer searches in an attempt to identify unknown fingerprints obtained at crime scenes and from physical evidence.

Ojai Bigfoot Afoot ?

Some high-tech bandits used nitroglycerine to blow up the post office safe in Ojai (still called Nordhoff in 1914) one night and escaped with $476. Nobody actually saw the robbers, but footprints found near the crime scene contained a shoe-print 11 inches long and 4-1/2 inches wide.

No strange tufts of hair from a "non-species-specific mammal" were found, so maybe it wasn't Bigfoot and his pals after all.

Okay. But I'm saying, what about clowns? Eh? Think about it.

Did an evil clown rob the Ojai Post Office safe?
Image: Library of Congress

(Thanks to longtime Santa Barbara "plugger" Bob Carlson who told me that the name Nordhoff was nixed during World War I because of anti-German sentiment.)

Looking Back, and Back Again

Newspaper readers 100 years ago here were looking back at the past just as we are today — at least all of you who are reading this book. One paper interviewed an 81-year-old man about changes he had seen over the decades. "I remember Santa Barbara when the streets were deep in sand, and the sidewalks were merely a string of planks leading from one store to another … Santa Barbara sure has been growing since then."

The same paper also contained a "blast from the past" column which noted that on April 4, 1856, the *Santa Barbara Gazette* had reported, "The projected lighthouse on Santa

The lighthouse on the Mesa was a picturesque sight from 1856 to 1925.

Image: *San Francisco Call,* December 13, 1896

Barbara point is about to be commenced. Mr. Nagle, the contractor, arrived on the *Sea Bird* and is already preparing the materials for its erection." The lighthouse was built on the Mesa and lasted nearly 70 years until the 1925 earthquake gave it the heave ho.

Read My Lips!

Ever wonder what the actors in silent films were really saying? Apparently not all kept to the script!

Some hearing-impaired people who could read lips fell over laughing in one theater during a death scene because they could tell that the actors' lines were not in keeping with the scene.

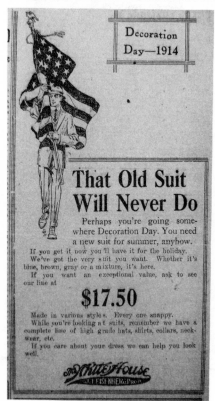

"Decoration Day" gradually morphed into "Memorial Day" during the 1900s.

Image: *Morning Press,* May 15, 1914

Memorial Day or Decoration Day?

Both names were used for the May 30th ceremony that was held in the Santa Barbara cemetery to honor those who had died in the armed forces. Ladies from the local veterans' support group went to the wharf and threw flowers into the water in remembrance of sailors who died at sea.

The holiday was originally called "Decoration Day" because people went to the cemeteries to decorate the graves of Civil War soldiers. By 1914, the papers here used both "Decoration Day" and "Memorial Day." May 30th was chosen because it was a time when many flowers were blooming. In 1967, the U.S. Government changed the name of the holiday to "Memorial Day." In 1971, the date of the holiday was changed to the last Monday in May.

Bombs Away! Far Away, Please!

Last month, I wrote about U.S. troop trains and warships passing through Santa Barbara on their way to the civil war in Mexico. This month, there was another local connection to the hostilities in the south. The front page of one of our papers held a photo of the French pilot Didier Masson who had dropped bombs over several cities in Mexico. (Masson was a mercenary working for the rebel side.) Fortunately Masson did not drop any bombs while he visited Santa Barbara, but perhaps if someone had paid him to do so, he might have.

Many Santa Barbarans would remember that Masson had landed his plane on the front lawn of the Potter Hotel on New Year's Day in 1911. (The hotel was located in the West Beach area.)

Image: *Daily News & Independent,* May 15, 1914

Long underwear was still commonplace in 1914, even in California – even in May!

Image: *Daily News & Independent,* May 16, 1914

Real Men — Bowl in Their Underwear?

Was this fellow on a coed team? Or was it come-as-you-are night for the guys? Union suits, so named because they united undershirts and underpants in one piece, were first patented in 1868. Normally, union suits (also called long johns) had a back flap to make for faster "pit stops," so I'm not sure why a closed crotch was a selling point. How did guys, um, … oh never mind.

The name Richmond was used because these undies were patented by the Richmond Underwear Company in Richmond, Indiana. In 1915, the company was bought by the Atlas Underwear Company which stayed in business long enough to manufacture "hi-tech metabolism-sensing long johns" used in Apollo missions' space suits.

The Atlas Underwear Company also owned the BVD company. BVD stands for Bradley, Voorhees & Day, an underwear company in New York. But you knew that, right? Atlas is no longer in business. Richmond, Indiana is still in business and is sometimes called the "cradle of recorded jazz" because some early jazz records were made there. I guess that sounds better than the "cradle of closed-crotch skivvies." Now, say that fast three times!

An Edhat reader commented on this article: the man in the advert is not bowling, he is probably in a gymnasium working out with a leather medicine ball. I only suspect this because we used to use one at gym in school when I was a wee lad!

Celebrity Sighting

Two of the largest actors from the Keystone Movie Company appeared in an exhibition baseball game in Santa Barbara. Marie Dressler was umpire, and Fatty Arbuckle, aka the "Human Roundhouse," played shortstop.

Roscoe "Fatty" Arbuckle weighed 13 pounds at birth when he was born in Kansas.

Image: courtesy of the Library of Congress

Apparently this was not the only time that Marie Dressler visited Santa Barbara. One Edhat reader wrote: Marie Dressler died in Santa Barbara; she was staying in one of the Billings' guest houses. Years ago there was an article in Santa Barbara Magazine *about Billings; one picture had Mr. B on his famous trotting horse Uhlan. Under the photo, it claimed Mrs. Billings was the woman standing beside the horse. My late friend, Margie Rupp, knew the Billings. She said, "That's Marie Dressler in the picture. Mrs. Billings would roll in her grave if she saw it."*

Everybody
Needs One
Everybody
Wants One

"Panama hats" come from Panama, and other urban myths.

Image: *Daily News & Independent,* May 23, 1914

Why Is This Dude Smiling?

What are you thinking that he wants? Hmmm… No, it wasn't that. And it wasn't a hug either. He's thinking about buying a spiffy new Panama hat, according to this ad from The Great Wardrobe. That store, located at 833 State Street, opened in 1886 and was one of the premier clothing stores in Santa Barbara through the 1940s.

Panama hats don't come really come from Panama — they are made in Ecuador. Why the name Panama? The hats are sent to Panama and shipped from there and, of course, once the Panama Canal opened, they must have been popular souvenirs.

(Spoiler alert! The canal was finished in August 1914.)

The opening of the canal, nicknamed "the Big Ditch," was eagerly awaited by all the cities on the California coast who realized it would mean more tourists and more business. The editorial in one of our papers enthused in especially awkward phraseology, "It will give the pleasure-seeker and those that in summer flee the heat-stricken Atlantic Coast, a delightful route to this land of delight, and … there doubtless will be many visitors to California, who never before would come in the summer, for dread of the long and uncomfortable journey overland."

Counting Down

There were a number of articles (pardon the pun) about numbers in May 1914:

The population of Santa Barbara reached an estimated **17,145** — an amazing increase of 50 percent since the census was taken in 1910. "The building permits show that a new home is going up almost every day, while many industrial and social buildings are in progress of construction," wrote one local paper. (In 2014, the estimated population was 89,082 according to the city's website.)

The "Fair View Ranch" containing more than **400** acres was being subdivided into nine ranches that contained 30 to 80 acres each. The land, near present-day Fairview Avenue, had been owned and farmed by Edgar Augustus Hollister. His father had owned the land since 1872.

One of the largest classes ever to graduate from Santa Barbara High School thus far was expected to number **53**. (In 2014, an estimated **460** students did the *Pomp and Circumstance* promenade.)

Advice from a Burglar?

He took the money and ran, but first he stopped to write an insulting note to his victim. Mrs. Sophia Parma of 912 Chapala Street returned home one day to find her house had been ransacked and $15 was stolen. The robber wrote, "Thanks for the 'dough.' Better keep your front door closed."

"Mrs. Parma admits that the front door of her house was left open this morning, and that the advice of the burglar is valuable," wrote the paper. It was not mentioned whether the police used their new fingerprinting equipment to finger the miscreant.

Sun in Eclipse

"The Guadalupe Sun [newspaper]… has ceased to shine, according to reports. The publication was formerly known as the *Moon*, but in the hope things might look a bit more brighter, the name was recently changed to the *Sun*."

I say the writer would have been a more successfuller writer if he/she had used better grammar. (Apologies to English teachers everywhere!)

There is still an S&H Green Stamps sign at the Santa Cruz Market in Goleta.

Image: Betsy J. Green

Remember S&H Green Stamps?

An ad for Krug Bros. Co. (431 State Street, phone Pacific 172), advertised Kentucky whiskey for $1 a quart and included S&H Green Stamps with each purchase. Krug Brothers also offered "Prompt Delivery," so if you ran out of hooch at an inopportune moment, you had only to pick up the phone.

The Krug Brothers' wine and liquor store was only here during the 19-teens. They were in competition with nine other liquor stores. (The brothers, Albert and Charles L. Krug, were not related to Charles Krug, founder of one of the first wineries in the Napa Valley in 1861.)

Okay, so what did S&H stand for? I sure didn't know, although I vaguely remember the little green stamps and the booklets you could trade in for stuff. The Sperry & Hutchinson Company began offering stamps to retailers back in 1896. They were popular through the 1960s, but are no longer used. The stamps were mentioned in a number of films and songs, most notably Pat Boone's 1962 hit *Speedy Gonzales* in which *Speedy Gonzales* (voiced by Mel Blanc) says, "Hey Rosita, come quick. Down at the cantina, they're giving green stamps with tequila." Did the lyricist get the idea from our very own Krug Bros?

This story caused one Edhat reader to contribute a paragraph from Wikipedia about the S&H Green Stamps story: Sperry and Hutchinson was sold by the founders' successors in 1981, and was purchased from a holding firm by a member of the founding Sperry family in 1999. At that time, only about 100 U.S. stores were offering Green Stamps. Eventually, the company modified its practices, and it now offers "greenpoints."

Female impersonators were hot in 1914 vaudeville shows in Santa Barbara.

Image: *Daily News & Independent,* May 2, 1914

Things Your Grandparents Never Told You!

A Mr. Finch wowed an audience of more than 700 people at the Mission Theatre on State Street one night in May. "Mr. Finch has a beautiful wardrobe and sings just like a woman," wrote one paper. The paper then announced that he/she would appear in drag the next day at a local store to see if anyone could tell who she/he was.

Well, dear readers, I know you just can't wait to learn whether he/she *was* outed or not. So I won't keep you in suspense. Mr. Finch *was* detected, in spite of his/her excellent gender disguise, and the woman — the genuine article, that is — who outed him received a $5 gift certificate. However, several other genuine specimens of the female persuasion present in the store were falsely accused of being imitations. Oh, the embarrassment! According to the paper, everyone "had a jolly time," but I imagine the falsely accused women went straight to the hat department and bought themselves a new chapeau to console their wounded pride. And who could blame them, darling?

If It's Good for Your Horse...

An ad for Snow Liniment claimed that it is "a healing remedy for all ailments of the flesh of man and beast." It was said to benefit two-legged creatures suffering from lacerated flesh, rheumatic pains, neuralgia, and sciatica. And it healed the sores and wounds of four-footed sufferers as well.

Judy Pearce, lifelong horsewoman, told me that it is quite common for people and horses to use the same product. She recalls a liniment that worked for her. "I remember using it on my horse when I was a kid, and when I had a sprained ankle I used it. … About 30 or so years ago, there was a product used on race horses, for their legs I believe, and some old man discovered rubbing it on the horse made the arthritis in his hands much better; well, that became a big deal and everyone wanted it." Pearce added that hair products are also used across species. "I remember when we realized cream conditioner used for horse's manes and tails would no doubt work for us too; we'd go to Jedlicka's to buy it; now it's sold in the grocery store with other hair products."

An investigation of the Snow liniment found that it contained turpentine and oil of horseradish. Maybe the smell distracted people from their aches and pains.

Image: *Morning Press,* May 2, 1914

Hotel Neal

The Hotel Neal at 217 State Street was requesting a permit that would allow the two-story building (shown in photo) to be increased by an additional floor. For more information about the Hotel Neal, I asked — who else? — Neal Graffy. He told me that the hotel was named for its first owner Neal Callahan. This hotel opened in 1906, and contained a restaurant and 29 rooms — some with a private bathroom; some not. It was located near the train station, and was an economical alternative to the pricier Potter Hotel on the ocean side of the tracks. The hotel did add a third floor in 1914. But due to extensive renovations after the 1925 quake, the present building looks quite different from the original.

Here's the Hotel Neal as it looked in 1906 before the addition of a third floor.

Image: courtesy of Neal Graffy

Get Ready! The End Is Near!

Okay, California doesn't have all the loonies in the world, but we do seem to have a healthy helping of crazies — now, and in the past. "Cultists Predict Destruction of Los Angeles; Flee by Boat" read the headline in the local paper. "Spurred by the belief that the southern metropolis is to be engulfed by destruction, a party of 147 Holy Lifers" stopped off at the wharf in Santa Barbara. One member of the "motley gathering" told the paper, "These are mighty days ... The prophecies are about to be fulfilled. The last seal is about to be broken. Destruction faces the world, and not only Los Angeles." The group then got back on the boat and continued north in search of who knows what.

image: Library of Congress

Laughing at History

Historical humor was always missing in any history class I ever had, so it's always a hoot to come across it in the Santa Barbara papers in 1914. Our city was cracking down on contractors hauling away sand from the beach to use on construction sites, and this inspired a satirical response from one of our papers.

"It is the plain duty of the city council to pass an ordinance to forbid the people taking water out of the ocean. Bathers should be compelled to wring their suits dry before leaving the surf. There's great danger of drying up the ocean. Also the wasteful practice of children playing in the sand, shoveling sand into buckets and otherwise needlessly handling it,

In addition to covering more skin, the swimsuits of 1914 absorbed more water.

Image: courtesy of the Library of Congress

should be discouraged. They wear out the sand by thus handling it. We must conserve 'our' ocean and 'our' sand."

It's interesting that the attitude in 1914 seemed to be that nature is limitless, in spite of the fact that in that year the last passenger pigeon, Martha, was nearing the end of her days — and her species — in a zoo in Cincinnati. And California sea otters were close to extinction as well.

So how about a joke that had 'em rolling in the aisles 100 years ago?

"Employee: Sir, I would respectfully ask you for an increase of salary. I have got married lately.

Manager: Very sorry … I can be of no assistance to you. The company is not responsible for any accidents that happen to its employees when off duty."

The Archduke Franz Ferdinand – the face that launched a thousand battles.

Image: courtesy of the Library of Congress

WAR!

The winds of war were starting in Europe, but here in Santa Barbara, the headlines at the end of June were more concerned with the civil war in Mexico. The assassination of the Archduke Franz Ferdinand of Austria was on the front page of the paper here, but clearly the implications of this event, which soon led to World War I, were not clear to citizens here. And we were not alone in this respect. A senior British lawyer quoted in the article said that the chances of peace in Europe were improved with the assassination because the Archduke's heir apparent leaned more toward peace than his dad who was killed. Oops! Got that one wrong!

Trivia Question of the Month

Anyone out there know what "pieplant" is? A recipe in the paper for "pieplant conserve" calls for cutting the pieplant in pieces and stewing it with sugar, orange rind, pineapple, and chopped almonds. What wouldn't taste good cooked like that, I ask you? (Pieplant's other name is revealed at the end of this month's chapter.)

A "lady of the evening" in New Orleans wearing killer tights.

Image: E.J. Bellocq

Sex at the Arlington Hotel!

No, that lady, er, that woman, was not what the story was about, dear readers. With neither fanfare nor smart-alecky comment, a local paper noted that one of the guests staying at the Arlington Hotel, the top hotel on Santa Barbara's State Street in 1914, was "James P. Sex, a well-known San Jose attorney." Thinking this must surely be a typo, I did a little digging, and found that, yes, Virginia, there was a lawyer named James P. Sex. He was an attorney who lived on Park Avenue in San Jose.

The 1913 edition of *Who's Who on the Pacific Coast*, lists James Patrick Sex, born in San Jose in 1875, as a criminal lawyer there. His family tree on Ancestry.com shows that his father, Peter Sex,

Around the Town

was born in Ireland. Why Sex, you may ask? According to *Irish Roots Magazine*, Sex may be a variant spelling of a surname that can be spelled Sisk, Seix, or Seys. James P. Sex died in 1926.

One Edhat reader (presumably a woman) coveted the striped stockings in the photo: I totally want a pair of those stockings! They're awesome!!

Bellosguardo Before the Clarks

This seaside estate originally belonged to the William Miller Graham family. The society column noted that Mrs. Graham gave an "al fresco affair" in June 1914. (When you live in a mansion, dear readers, you don't have "picnics," you have "al fresco affairs." Remember that when your ship comes in and you move into a mansion. And I hope you'll remember to invite me to your "al fresco affair." I'll bring the kale chips.)

And you must remember to give your mansion a fancy name that most people cannot pronounce properly. (*Maid of Plywood* or *The Loan Ranger* will *not* cut it as mansion

monikers.) *Bellosguardo* is pronounced BELL-os-GWAR-doe, according to author Bill Dedman who penned the recent best-seller *Empty Mansions*. In the book, he notes that the Grahams are the ones who built the original 25,000-square-foot Italian villa here in 1903. The Clarks did a major teardown/rebuild after the 1925 quake.

"Fire Threatens Chinese Quarter"

This headline described a fire at the Kay Fong grocery store in our city's Chinatown. "The fire was extinguished before extensive damage had been done." According to the 1915-16 city directory at the Gledhill Library in the Historical Museum, Kay Fong & Co. was located at 11 East Cañon Perdido. It was one of 16 Chinese busineses that were located on East Cañon Perdido.

This was one of the many businesses in our thriving Chinatown.
Image: courtesy of John C. Woodward

The Channel Islands' sea lions were popular with zoos around the world.

Image: Gary R. Osgood

A Seal of Approval

According to an article in 1914, "The sea lion industry at Santa Barbara has developed quite a lively activity. This morning Captain Vasquez brought in five splendid specimens, and yesterday, Captain Ira K. Eaton delivered several. ... Between Captain Vasquez and Captain Eaton, the demand for sea lions is being supplied steadily. Shipments are made to all parts of the country and to Europe, and prove quite an advertisement to the Santa Barbara islands."

The sea lions of 1914 were shipped off to zoos. They were more fortunate than their ancestors. The Channel Islands' sea lions of the 1800s were captured and killed for their pelts and blubber. According to Marla Daily of the Santa Cruz Island Foundation, "Sealing as an industry developed around the Channel Islands as whaling declined." But by 1910, killing seals was no longer permitted.

Marla is hard at work constructing *Islapedia*, an online encyclopedia with everything you wanted to know about the California Channel Islands. "Keeping island history alive and bringing the dead to life."

Several Edhat readers agreed with the one who wrote: Couldn't make it through the seal article. Made my heart hurt... :(

The sultry Leah Baird appeared in The Flaming Diagram *here in 1914.*

Image: *Stars of Photoplay*

What Did People Do Before TV?

Well, that was before my time. (And yours too, right?) But, judging from the ads in the 1914 newspapers here, they went to the movies – *a lot!* The Mission Theatre ("We Lead, Others Follow") on State Street advertised that it was showing new movies every day. So, if you wanted to catch your favorite star (such as the one above), you had to go to the movie theater on June 3, 1914, or forget about it.

Sorry, Mister Snake!

An article in June about the Santa Barbara Hikers group encountering the first rattlesnake of the season, which was promptly killed, led me to wonder when trail users began treating our snake population with a little more consideration. I asked Dave Everett, author of the forthcoming book *Rediscovering the Trails of Mission Canyon*. He told me that "the unwritten policy in the late 1800s and early 1900s was, 'the only good rattlesnake was a dead rattlesnake.' Trails users wouldn't think twice about killing a rattler upon first sight. When creating their bylaws, the Hikers considered allowing members to carry firearms, but decided against it, citing the only reason it would be useful was when encountering a rattlesnake." Dave added that it wasn't until the 1960s, that most people started thinking about living with rattlers, instead of killing as many as possible.

An Edhat reader commented: I am SO GLAD we no longer kill rattlesnakes just because they may harm us. Now we know their value for rodent control.

Forbidden Fruits for Sale on State Street!

The Diehl Grocery at 827 State Street (Phone 44) declared that June 1 to June 7 was "Fresh Currant" week at their establishment. Currants are not as common as other berries today and here's why: Currants (*Ribes sp.*) weren't forbidden fruits back in 1914, but for many years, it was illegal to grow them in certain counties in California and in numerous other areas elsewhere in the United States. (In my misspent youth, I was a staff editor at *World Book Encyclopedia* and one of the articles I worked on — and still remember — was the currant article.) So anyway, what's the problem with currants? The currant plant is a host for the white pine blister rust, a fungus that kills pine trees. In areas where the lumber industry is important to the economy, it is illegal to sell or plant currant bushes.

The first light bulbs were lit in Carpinteria in 1914.

Image: Ulfbastel

Let There Be Light!

The good folks in Carp were not "on the grid" yet in 1914. "Active work on the construction of the power line to Carpinteria is to begin at once, the Santa Barbara Gas & Electric Company agreeing to complete the line within 30 days, and it is expected that before the end of the present month, Carpinteria will be receiving electricity from the Santa Barbara plant."

Trivia Question Answer

Rhubarb used to be called pieplant because it was often used as a pie filling.

This brought back some happy memories for one Edhat reader: I remember being 4-5 years old and my Mom giving me a stalk of rhubarb to chew on, while she shopped at Santa Cruz Market on Milpas.

Way Back When IN SANTA BARBARA

July 4th Celebration a Big Success!

Unlike the oopsie! we experienced at the Santa Barbara fireworks in 2014, things went off with a bang in 1914. Granted, they did things a little differently 100 years ago when there were fewer lawyers in California. A raft was moored about a mile offshore with a 10-pound charge of dynamite and a container of gasoline which was set ablaze. (Who volunteered for that job?) "When the oil had burnt its way down to the dynamite, there ensued an explosion that made one big commotion that carried joy to the ears of those who dote on a noise for the 4th of July." You can't go wrong with dynamite and gasoline, I always say! They really knew how to party back then.

Don't try this at home, kids!
Image: courtesy of the Library of Congress

Tightest Jeans Award?

The morning parade on the 4th featured a $50 prize for the "best-equipped cowboy." (Double entendre probably not intended back in 1914.) Another eyebrow-raising item in the paper was an ad for the *Climax* Grocery Store at 1037 State Street. Today, that approximate address is occupied by the Business First Bank. Hmmm. Business first? What's second? Pleasure?

There was also a parade of 500 automobiles decorated with lanterns that drove from the Arlington Hotel at State and Victoria streets down to the beach. An estimated 15,000 people enjoyed the festivities that day. Some 2,500 had arrived from Ventura on two special trains. The morning parade included a few — a very few — veterans of the Civil War that had ended almost 50 years earlier. "Most of the veterans refused to ride and sturdily marched, while those who could not, occupied three prettily decorated automobiles." The paper added morbidly, "This is probably the last time the G.A.R. [Grand Army of the Republic — Civil War veterans of the Union Army] will take such a conspicuous part in any celebration here," and predicted that many of them would not be around for the next July 4th celebration.

The Japanese Roof Garden Restaurant was a popular spot in 1914.

Image: courtesy of Neal Graffy

The dynamite display in the channel would have made a great show for the people who were spending the evening at the Japanese Roof Garden restaurant on the corner of Cabrillo Boulevard and Castillo Street: "Where the Cooling Breezes Blow." In true melting-pot fashion, you could watch U.S. Independence Day activities from a Japanese-décor restaurant in a Mission-style building "near the Plaza del Mar."

Sapho's star Florence Roberts was a serious stage actress who made only a handful of films.

Image: courtesy of the Library of Congress

First X-rated Movie in Santa Barbara?

Perhaps. The Hollywood rating system had not been invented, but the Mission Theater on State Street was not allowing unaccompanied minors to view the four-reel movie *Sapho*. (Among other things, the main character has a child out of wedlock.) This restriction was in spite of the fact that the paper noted that "the censorship board has eliminated all objectionable features … there is nothing of the objectionable character in the play. Many of Santa Barbara's leading citizens saw the play last night and no one was heard to criticize it."

On The Town

This adobe was once located about where Dargan's Pub is today.
Image: courtesy of John C. Woodward

Another Adobe Bites the Dust (Pun intended!)

"Adobe to Make Way for Garage," read the headline. Now if that doesn't spell *Progress*, I don't know what does. Pretty close to "pave paradise and put up a parking lot," eh? "Another old adobe landmark is about to disappear and make room for a modern structure," noted the local paper. "The building will be one story, of brick, with a frontage of 40 feet and extending about 100 feet back." The paper added that the adobe was, well, old. "The old adobe now on the property was probably erected about the same time as the De la Guerra mansion, when Santa Barbara was little more than Presidio. For many years, it has been used for storage purposes, and its exterior has served somewhat as a billboard, so there will probably be no hue and cry about its destruction."

Oh, Pearl Chase! Where were you when we needed you? Actually, she was here, but had not yet started her campaign to spruce up Santa Barbara, according to Cheri Rae, author of the book *Pearl Chase: First Lady of Santa Barbara*.

Santa Barbara historian Neal Graffy (who is always here when we need him) is very familiar with this building. "That shop … was at 18 E. Ortega Street and was run by Horace A. Sexton and C. Phillip Reynolds. By 1921, Reynolds was gone … and it was Sexton's Garage. The following year … the business was Sexton and Simpson until 1938 when it became H. C. Simpson's garage, and it closed in 1942ish. There is currently a nice old brick building at 18 E. Ortega doing business as Dargan's Irish Pub. Undoubtedly the same place. I'm sure there's a joke in here somewhere about automobiles and alcohol — from lubing cars to lubing patrons?"

Clubbing Around Town

Two buildings that were newly constructed in 1914 are still with us today. "Polo Club to Have Attractive Montecito Home," ran the headline announcing the beginning stages of construction of the clubhouse. I asked Hattie Beresford, Montecito historian and writer, about this. "The article is referring to the Bartlett Polo Field which once took up a significant number of lots in the Montecito Land Company's subdivision surrounding Middle Road … It was built by William Bartlett. The clubhouse was designed by Underhill. After the polo club closed, the clubhouse became a home. It still exists today, but has been heavily remodeled into a modern home."

The Recreation Center was one of the few brick buildings in the city to survive the 1925 earthquake.

Image: courtesy of Neal Graffy

The newly constructed Recreation Center on Carrillo and Anacapa streets was getting ready to open its 850-seat auditorium. The seating seemed to be the star of the show, according to one article. "The chairs are roomy and do not shake or collapse … Neither do the chairs squeak, and they are tasteful." The Recreation Center was indeed well built. It would survive the 1925 earthquake and moreover served as an emergency shelter in the quake's aftermath.

Peter, the movie dog, was generally well behaved. Until one day …

Image: courtesy of Dana Driskel

Bad Dog!

Peter the movie dog did a naughty thing during the Flying A's filming of *Suspended Ceremony*. No, not the kind of naughty thing that necessitates a 15-minute cleanup and half a roll of paper towels. No, Peter actually followed his instincts, and he thought he was being a Good Dog! As part of the action in the film, the actor, who was Peter's owner and trainer in real life, was thrown into the lake. Peter, who, like some people, had trouble differentiating between Real Life and Art (or Real Life and Reel Life) jumped into the lake and "rescued" his owner. Oops! CUT!

Mmm, Mmm Good!

An ad for Campbell's soups caught my eye in a July 1914 newspaper. Among the 15 varieties listed was "Printanier." That was a new one for me, so I asked my French friend Danielle Levi-Alvares. She had heard of the soup whose name refers to spring — "it is a vegetable soup, but light and with spring veggies … the ingredients would be peas, baby carrots, celery and maybe zucchinis." But she did not recall ever seeing it on a menu and could find no recipe for it in her big French cookbook. "Not a good sign," she said. Ah well, it was probably too hard to spell.

Mountain lions are a protected species now.
Image: courtesy of the Library of Congress

From Rattlesnakes to Mountain Lions

Faithful readers of my Edhat column (you know who you are), especially those who can remember stuff from one month to the next, will recall that for my June 1914 *Way Back When* column, I had a story about hikers killing rattlers. Well, in July 1914, mountain lions were in the crosshairs. The lions were said to be "ravaging the corrals" in Toro Canyon. A $25 bounty was offered. "The residents of the canyon will be pleased to witness the slaughter of the marauders," commented the local paper.

Today the California Department of Fish and Game's website states that: "With the passage of Proposition 117 in 1990, mountain lions became a 'specially protected species,' making mountain lion hunting illegal in California. ...It is illegal to take, injure, possess, transport, import, or sell any mountain lion or part of a mountain lion. Mountain lions may be killed only 1) if a depredation permit is issued to take a specific lion killing livestock or pets; 2) to preserve public safety; or 3) to protect listed bighorn sheep."

Livery Stables in Santa Barbara

An ad for a livery business caught my eye in a July 1914 paper. Today, the word "livery" is seen on limo license plates, but few other places. Liveries, usually called livery stables, were places that boarded and rented horses and carriages. The Overland Livery, at 114 East Carrillo Street in the ad I noticed, rented hearses! and carriages as well as "gentle horses for ladies and children, for either riding or driving." That got me wondering — how long were there livery stables in downtown Santa Barbara? I let my fingers do the walking through the old city directories in the public library, and discovered that there were nine livery stables in the business listings in 1914, only three in the 1929-30 directory, and only one in 1938 — the last year that "Livery and Boarding Stables" was a category in the business listings.

It's not surprising that horseless carriages eventually replaced the horse-powered variety. What *was* surprising, however, was that the man who was listed as having the last livery stable Santa Barbara in 1938, had also been listed in the 1914 directory — 24 years earlier! His name was Frank Reasons. In his long obituary in 1954, the paper noted that, "No one in Santa Barbara was better qualified to supply horses … in this city … His influence in the riding game in Santa Barbara history was considered far-reaching."

Four years after Reasons' death, the city declared his livery stable a fire hazard. His widow, and other people such as Lutah Maria Riggs, tried to save it as the bulldozers closed in for the kill, but I could find no record of it being saved. Reasons' livery barn was located at 518 Anacapa Street, between Haley and Cota streets. Today, that address is home to an auto body and paint business. From a horse barn to an auto body shop — *sic transit livery stables!*

Edhat reader and vintage photo collector John Woodward added: The first Sanborn map to show it was the 1892 where it is called "Billy Sproul's Livery & Feed" at 516 Anacapa St.

Watching a Fiesta parade is way more interesting than any board game.

Image: courtesy of the Library of Congress

Was There Life Before Fiesta?

Well, we celebrated/survived the 90th anniversary of Fiesta in 2014. That means that 100 years ago – August 1914 – we were Fiesta-free. Was there life in Santa Barbara before Fiesta? Before we had Fiesta, we had … um, well … not much, actually. There were chess and checker games at the new Y.M.C.A. on Carrillo and Chapala streets. If you didn't know how to play, you could always watch, right? Now doesn't *that* sound like fun?

The Women's Auxiliary of the G.A.R. (a veterans' group) held a "dime social" at the home of one of their members. Santa Barbara historian Kathi Brewster told me that

dime socials were potlucks at which guests paid 10 cents for each spoonful that they took from the buffet table. Or how about a "thimble party"? Ladies who sewed (remember sewing?) could bring their sewing projects to the party and sew stuff together. Okay, who remembers what a thimble is? And over at the Baptist Church, there was a watermelon social, where you could, I guess, eat watermelon. Well, you know how some things *always* taste better when you're with friends, eh?

So, that's what life was like here in August in 1914. No wonder Fiesta sounded like a good idea ten years later in 1924!

One Edhat reader wanted to know: Have only faint memories of the YMCA at Chapala and Carrillo Street. What building went in after that?

And another Edhatter provided a quick and informed reply: The old YMCA building at Carrillo & Chapala was razed and the property is now the site of Ralph's supermarket.

Nuts to Panama!

The opening of the Panama Canal, nicknamed "the big ditch," was a major milestone in 1914.

Image: courtesy of the New York Public Library

According to a local paper, "In the first cargo to go through the Panama Canal, will be walnuts from Goleta. These nuts have already been delivered here and the sacks are objects of much interest at the wharf because of the fact that they go on this initial voyage, which signals the opening of the canal to freight steamers." Now that's something Goleta folks can brag about.

Beach Crowds Enjoy Weird Spectacle

No, it wasn't a cardboard kayak race or bathing suits that ended above the knee – it was an eerie green glow in the water described as "a spectacle beautiful in the extreme. ... Large crowds of people gather on the wharves and along the seashore nightly to wonder at and enjoy the fascinating sight. ... The agitation of the water from any cause – moving fishes or boats, dipping oars or anything else that stirs the water – causes a showing of the most exquisite emerald color that could be imagined."

I asked a number of Santa Barbarans if they'd ever seen this, but none had. So, I contacted Milton Love, research biologist at UCSB, and author of *Certainly More Than You Want to Know about the Fishes of the Pacific Coast* to get his expert explanation. He told me, "This probably happens every year to a greater or lesser degree. The bioluminescence that we see in the water is caused by dinoflagellates, very small organisms that form much of the plankton. When one of these tiny organisms is disturbed, by being pushed about in the water for instance, it flashes a tiny bit of blue-green light. Why these organisms do that is not completely understood." He added that lightning bugs are another kind of bioluminescent creature.

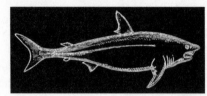

A couple of Edhat readers said they have seen the phosphorescence, but not in Santa Barbara: If you have ever been at sea on a large ship, particularly a warship running without lights for safety, you will often see the emerald green glow in the wake of the ship caused by the screws churning up the water.

And another: Living in the SB area since 1957, first IV near the beach which I was often on night swims I've never seen the green glow, but for a short while I lived in Santa Monica a couple blocks from the beach and a party full of us would go down to the ocean, form a ring and kick vigorously, creating an intense green glowing circle of light.

Image: courtesy of the Library of Congress

My Dears! Have You Been to the New El Mirasol Hotel?

It is simply *la crème de la crème*, if you catch my drift. "A rare artistic treat awaits those who have been asked to attend the formal opening," opined one society columnist. However, due to disturbed conditions resulting from the war in Europe," (Silly old war! That can't last long, can it, darling?) only the restaurant and tearoom were available. Accommodations for overnight guests were not open until November. According to a local paper, "No more beautiful setting for social affairs could possibly be desired than this wonderful new hostelry."

Hattie Beresford, Santa Barbara historian, has written that the hotel was originally the private home of Mary Miles Herter, which had been built only a few years before. In the late 1960s, the hotel was torn down and eventually morphed into Alice Keck Park Memorial Gardens. The sandstone wall of the Herter home still rims the property.

(continued on next page)

Hueter Residence
Santa Barbara, Cal.

This article about the El Mirasol Hotel created numerous comments, questions, and answers from curious and informed Edhat readers:

Why was the lovely El Mirasol torn down?

The El Mirasol was the site of a development battle when a local realtor (Bill Hackett) and investors sought to build high-rise condominiums there, which would have been a precedent for high-rise (over 9 stories) in downtown Santa Barbara. It was eventually defeated and is now the Alice Keck Park (Park and Gardens).

Great article, Betsy, as usual. If I recall correctly, our own Pearl Chase fought the battle with local developers who wanted to replace The El Mirasol with a gigantic hotel.

Thank the gods that Pearl Chase and many others fought against the high-rise condos.

As for Alice Keck Park Park, my dear friend, Estelle Busch, since passed on, was one who fought tooth and nail to keep condos off that land. Remember when there was a huge organic garden? Passion fruit and lots of other delicious foods were grown there.

My grandmother died at El Mirasol Hotel about 1943-44 and many years later my husband worked for CEC at the organic gardens on that spot.

Thanks, as always, for your wonderful column. I remember going to El Mirasol on several occasions for dinner and once, to a lovely wedding reception. It was a beautiful and gracious hotel with lovely grounds.

Betsy, thanks for another of your fantastic reports. Mom was 2 years old in 1914, Grandma 23; I like pictures and articles of how things were then.

A good history of the El Mirasol - from park to home to hotel to condo project to garden and finally back to park can be found in the book Santa Barbara, Then and Now. *[Gee! I wonder who posted this last anonymous comment? Could it be what's-his-name the author?]*

---

left: The El Mirasol Hotel was the newest place to see and be seen when it opened on August 18, 1914.

right: The stone wall around Alice Keck Park Memorial Gardens is a reminder of the El Mirasol Hotel.

Images: courtesy of Neal Graffy's latest book *Santa Barbara, Then and Now*

Residence of Valentine Hall, 2029 Castillo St.; C. W. Northrop, builder.

It's still here! Unlike the El Mirasol Hotel, which is long gone, there was a bungalow built in 1914 that is still here.

Image: *Daily News & Independent*, July 14, 1914

A Bungalow with Staying Power

When I look through the 1914 papers each month for this column, I often see references to new homes being built, but when I check the addresses to see if they're still around, they're often gone. So, I was happy to find one featured in the paper in August 1914 that's still around and still looks much the same as it did 100 years ago. Happy anniversary, 2029 Castillo Street house! (Please do not disturb the current residents.)

Image: *Morning Press*, 1914

One hundred years and counting – the 2029 Castillo Street home is still here.

Image: Betsy J. Green

The home was built for Valentine Hall, who shared the home with his mother and later his wife Eva and two children. Hall was a telegraph operator for the Southern Pacific Railroad. His mother was the manager of the postal telegraph office here in Santa Barbara. I wonder if they planted the tree.

I was not the only one who was happy to find a 100-year-old bungalow in such great shape. Other Edhat readers were pleased as well: WOW Betsy, great piece. Can't believe how little that one remaining house has changed. Please keep the articles coming. I really like your style.

Last year I walked down Castillo Street and passed 2029. Even after living here for 25 years, I never noticed the jacaranda tree in the front yard.

Thanks for posting, that jacaranda has to be one the biggest in SB.

Another wonderful and enlightening column, fantastic work! That jacaranda is, to my mind, one of the largest and finest in SB. Wonderful to read about the bungalow. Do not disturb, indeed, but I'm sure the people who live there appreciate it, and much other art.

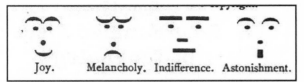

Emoticons are probably as old as typewriters. These date to 1881.

Image: courtesy of *Puck*, March 30, 1881

"Oh, Cheer Up!"

Such was the headline of an editorial about the beginning of [spoiler alert!]World War I in a local paper. "After a good scrap or two," the editorial continued, "the Europeans will come to their senses. Why, bless you, they can't keep the thing up long."

Originally, I was going to end that paragraph with the words "wink, wink" since I assumed that emoticons such as ;) or :-D had not been invented yet, but when I did a little research, I discovered that people were creating emoticons on typewriters as far back as the 1800s.

But despite the :-D tone of the local editorial, Santa Barbarans were beginning to feel :{ about the growing conflict "across the pond" by the beginning of August. Residents with friends or relatives traveling in Europe worried about their safety and wondered when they could return home. (Steamship companies had cancelled service indefinitely.) "With no present prospect of trans-Atlantic travel, and with practically all communications with other countries cut off, the whereabouts and condition of Santa Barbarans on the continent will cause serious apprehension here until reassuring news is heard from them," noted one local paper.

Fortunately, among the Santa Barbarans stranded on the other side of the Atlantic was Sarah Redington, a writer for one of our newspapers. She rose to the occasion and wrote several long articles for the paper about her predicament. "Things have happened with such astounding suddenness ... Friday morning, we were tourists; Friday night, we were refugees; today, I am not quite sure what we ought to call ourselves." She and her traveling companions were forced to leave their luggage in Paris, and make a mad dash for one of the last boats crossing the channel to England. [Spoiler alert – Sarah eventually returned to Santa Barbara. In a future column, I will tell you how and when she got back.]

Fingerprinting was a boon for local enforcement agencies.
Image: Metrónomo

Someday My Prints Will Come!

In my *Way Back When* column for April 1914, I wrote about the Santa Barbara police acquiring what they called a "finger-marking system," or what we would call fingerprinting equipment. In August, the new equipment was used to help the police avoid locking up an innocent man. The police in Long Beach had sent the police here a description of a man wanted for robbery, along with his photo and prints. "One of the force at the local police station, after a careful scrutiny of the photograph and general description, declared ... that he had seen the man only half an hour before. The chief told the officer to 'bring him in.'" The suspect strongly protested his innocence, so the police took an impression of his fingerprints and compared them to the prints from Long Beach. They were radically different. Whew! The muchly relieved prisoner was immediately released. Ya gotta love technology, eh?

Are cats more intelligent than dogs?

Image: courtesy of the Library of Congress

Smarty Cat!

Last month, I wrote about Peter the movie dog who ruined a shot when he rescued someone who was not supposed to be rescued. My animal story this month is about a cat who did not seem to merit a name, but did earn a fairly lengthy story in a local paper. The tabby cat lived with the Kellogg family at 1715 Anacapa Street (the home is no longer there – you can see why I got excited about the bungalow a couple of pages earlier). One night, after the family had gone to bed, the cat sat under the bedroom window and meowed. Mr. Kellogg went to the door to let the cat in. Instead of heading in, the cat ran back and forth on the porch. Mr. Kellogg returned to bed, probably mumbling some unkind words about felines. A short time later, he heard another noise outside and he got up to investigate. When he looked outside, he discovered a horse that he had sold to someone else a few months before. The horse had wandered back home, and the cat – dare I say, a tattle tail – was trying to convey that message. I hope the cat got an extra helping of kitty love the next morning.

Edhat cat people had questions and answers: The stripe pattern on that cat is REALLY cool - can't help but wonder if that's what tabby cats usually looked like back then, and if so, how and why they morphed into the smaller stripes we commonly see nowadays.

Another Edhat reader answered: There are different types of tabbies. The one in the picture is a Classic Tabby (also called Bullseye Tabby). The more common one with the smaller stripes is a Mackerel Tabby.

Interesting article as always, Betsy! Tabby info in the comments were appreciated too!

Another New-Fangled Piece of Technology

A first for Santa Barbara in 1914 was a "canned" speech by a politician recorded on a dictaphone record that was delivered to women's groups all over Southern California. "The home of Mrs. Frank Maguire [1721 Garden Street – still here! Whoopee! Found another one!] will be the scene of an interesting political meeting … when possibly for the first time in history, the dictaphone will be brought into service as a vehicle through which a typical campaign speech is to be made." The candidate, Congressman Joseph R. Knowland, was running for the U.S. Senate.

Dictaphones originally recorded onto wax cylinders, but by 1914, 12-inch discs were used. One side benefit (pun intended!) was that the record could only hold a speech fewer than five minutes long!

image: New York Public Library

Botanic Garden Bench & Library Lore

Just before I sat down at my writing desk on Sunday with quill and ink (well, actually it was my laptop on ye olde kitchen table), I went for a ramble through the shady groves of the Botanic Garden after the rain so that I could remember what wet plants looked like. I chose the Pritchett Trail because you are rewarded with a nice ocean view at the top, and usually a bit of breeze. Along the way, I noticed a bench with a thoughtful quotation written by a Mr. Pritchett, "The way of truth is along the path of intellectual sincerity." I had no idea who he was at the time. After my walk, as I started to shuffle through my August 1914 clippings, his name popped out at me.

Back in 1914, Henry Smith Pritchett lived at 320 Junipero Plaza in Santa Barbara, and was president of the Carnegie Foundation. This organization donated money to build public libraries in towns all over the United States. There were almost 1,700 nationwide, including 142 in California. Only 85 of the 142 are still standing proud-

A preliminary design for the library ran on page one.

Image: *Morning Press,* August 28, 1914

ly, and ours is one. There was a Carnegie library in Santa Maria, but it was torn down in 1969. Lompoc's Carnegie library is now home to the Lompoc Museum.

The Carnegie Foundation provided $50,000 for our library in 1914 – a move which was considered unusual by the local paper, "In granting Santa Barbara $50,000 for a library building, the Carnegie Foundation trustees have broken their long-established rule to give no more money to cities …" Perhaps, just perhaps, they broke the rule because Pritchett and another trustee of the Foundation were residents here. But anyway, we got the money and the local paper cheered, "Santa Claus is coming our way in advance of Christmas."

So back to the Botanic Garden. I contacted the garden's director Steve Windhager who steered me to a history of the garden written by Mary Carroll. After Henry S. Pritchett died in 1939, his widow Eva donated money to create the trail and construct the bench with one of his sayings. Look for it the next time you visit the garden.

This article caused one Edhat reader to take a closer look at something we see all the time, but rarely notice: How interesting that our library is a Carnegie library! Naturally the board of the foundation broke their own rules just this once… shocking, unheard of… All the other Carnegie libraries I've seen are in small towns and "neoclassical" in style. The old front door of our library is so gorgeous and nowadays so easy to overlook on Anapamu St.

The original main door of our library is worth looking for.

Image: Betsy J. Green

Attention, ladies! Here's how you would have wowed 'em way back when.
Image: courtesy of the Library of Congress

Attention-Getting Fashion at the Beach

"A new bathing suit that will doubtless attract much attention when it first dips into the ocean is made of white embroidered taffeta. The embroidery is done in red, in the design of small sea urchins and shrimps, which form an appropriate but weird banding. Red and white shoes, hat, cape, and parasol go with it." Taffeta? Really? What did it look like *after* you came out of the water?

Guys were luckier – as always. Their bathing suits were simpler and looked like you could actually swim in them. And if they were really lucky, they owned their own swimsuits. The not-so-lucky guys rented swimsuits that God-knows-how-many-other-guys had worn. Ewww!

The White House, a Santa Barbara clothing store, asked in an ad: "You wouldn't wear another man's clothes at home, why should you at the shore? Our offerings this season are the latest color combinations in knit bathing suits. … Bathing Caps, Bathing Shoes, Bathing Hosiery, and Water Wings." *Bathing Hosiery!* Really? And we call them the good old days?

To Hell and Back

The articles in Santa Barbara newspapers were read by folks all over the county. Here's a letter to the editor of the *Lompoc Journal* about an article in our local paper (August 8, 1914).

"I presume that you saw in the *Santa Barbara Press* and other papers an account of the lady who, in a recent illness hovering on the verge of death, actually experienced a foretaste of the life beyond the grave."

The writer then described his or her own trip Down There and back during a severe health problem. "On entering the pit, I was met by a lot of little imps with three-pronged spears. They seemed to lift me onto a mass of burning brimstone, while the other little imps shoveled on more sulphur. As I lay and roasted, every bad thing I had ever done and every bad word I had ever uttered flashed through my mind like a streak of lightning, and oh, how I wished I had lived a better life. No one can imagine the suffering I went through."

The writer concludes, "As I sat roasting and praying for a return to life again, I awoke and found it was only a dream." Unfortunately, the writer does not mention whether he/she mended his/her ways, or continued down the road to perdition.

WAY BACK WHEN IN SANTA BARBARA

Travel author N.H. Chittenden called Santa Barbara his home.

Image: *Morning Press,* Sept. 10, 1914

Mule Man (ver. 1.0) Makes an Appearance

Guess what! Our present-day 2014 Mule Man is not the original. The original Mule Man in our area was Newton Henry Chittenden who first passed through our fair city in 1871 when he was 32. He was here to celebrate his 75th birthday on September 10, 1914. Chittenden considered himself a Santa Barbara resident, although he spent most of his time on the road. The local paper wrote that Chittenden "has devoted most of his time to roaming about the country and especially the West ... He has crossed the continent 34 times in the last century."

Not only did the Mule Man (ver. 1.0) crisscross the country, he somehow found time to write more than 25 travel books with such tongue-twisting titles as, *Settlers, Miners and Tourists Guide From Ocean to Ocean by the Canadian Pacific Railroad, the Great Trans-Continental Short Line Through a Region of Unsurpassed Attractions for Settler, Miner and Tourist; Homes, Health and Pleasure in Southern California;* and *Among the Cocopahs ...*

Okay, I give up! What the heck are Cocopahs? Sounds like a breakfast cereal to me. What do I know?

So, of course, I looked up them up and discovered that they are a group of Native Americans in Arizona numbering almost 1,000. So now you know. My apologies to Cocopahs everywhere.

One sharp-eyed Edhat reader, who is more knowledgeable about our four-footed friends than I am, wrote to tell me that the animal pictured with "Mule Man" is actually a donkey. I loved the alliteration of Mule Man, but I guess I should have called him "Donkey Dude."

And many thanks to the Edhat reader who actually knew the Mule Man / Donkey Dude and shared his/her memory with Edhat: "I remember the gent in the Mule Man photo, Newton Chittenden. He used to live on East Montecito Street and we all referred to him as "Captain," although he was practicing law at the time. He'd fought in the Civil War, reaching the rank of 1st Lieutenant, although I always thought maybe he'd been discharged with the rank of Captain, hence the nickname. During his last years, he was in the Old Soldiers' Home in Los Angeles and that's where he ultimately succumbed.

AMONG THE COCOPAHS.

BY CAPT. NEWTON H. CHITTENDEN.

FIFTY miles east of Tia Juana, Mexico, at the picturesque mountain border station of Campo, on the early U. S. mail and emigrant road between Fort Yuma and San Diego, I exchanged my gentle Mexican pack pony for an untrained, vicious little burro, as the only beast of burden which could survive an extended desert journey. It began service by bucking off the saddle, charging through the chaparral and cactus, scattering my outfit, tearing corduroys, lacerating the flesh, provoking strong language and permanently impairing confidence. But this wonderful specimen of animated nature was finally persuaded to carry my blankets and provisions five hundred and forty-five miles, over the

Walking Barefoot Around the World!

September 1914 certainly saw some crazies pass through Santa Barbara. Not only did we have a visit from the Mule Man, but Rattlesnake Jim also stopped here for a spell on his journey around the world – barefoot. He said he was from Switzerland, and his name was James Lauhno Lonefeather. He claimed that his father was a Sioux Indian and his mother was Swiss. He said he'd been walking barefoot for 17 years in order to "obtain three-important things – an education better than any university can furnish, a health that is immune to any disease, and adventures that are impossible for many to find."

A website that contains numerous newspaper articles about this colorful character concludes that although Jim seems to have walked from the East Coast to the West Coast, other parts of his story might be more creative than realistic.

My question is this: Did the Mule Man and Rattlesnake Jim meet up here while they were both in Santa Barbara? Wouldn't you love to have been a fly on the wall at their encounter?

Depositors line up on the first day at the New York Postal Bank.

Image: courtesy of the Library of Congress

When the Post Office Doubled as a Bank

In September 1914, Santa Barbarans had deposited more than $18,000 in postal savings bank deposits. From 1911 until 1966, the United States Post Offices operated as banks. The U.S. Postal Savings System paid two percent interest. According to Wikipedia, "The system originally had a natural advantage over deposit-taking private banks because the deposits were always backed by 'the full faith and credit of the United States Government.'" But once the Federal Deposit Insurance Corporation began guaranteeing deposits in banks, the Post Office banking system lost some of its appeal.

The paper noted, "The local bank at the post office now has over 500 accounts, many of which have been started by laboring men, who find the hours the bank is open more suited to their needs, than those of the ordinary savings banks."

One Edhat reader wrote to say that two percent interest sounded like a pretty good idea in 2014.

A Stamp of Approval for Mailboxes

(Pun intended!) A large notice by Postmaster Thomas M. Storke appeared in the papers here announcing that mail carriers would no longer deliver mail to rear or side doors of homes or businesses. "The action is taken in order to save carriers as much time as possible." Residents were encouraged to purchase sheet-metal mailboxes (only 15¢) approved by the Post Office. (I hope everyone appreciates the time and effort it took me to figure out how to insert the ¢ symbol in this story. There used to be a ¢ key on typewriters way back when. Ah, Progress!)

Did it come to this? Say it isn't so!
Image: *Popular Science Monthly, vol. 56*

"Dynamite May Be Used to Blow Open Post Office Safe"

Well, that headline caught my attention. We had a fine show of dynamite and gasoline on July 4th, 1914, but that was out in the channel on a raft, not in the Post Office on State Street. (The Santa Barbara Museum of Art now occupies what was the old Post Office Building.)

The newspaper explained, "Several days ago, the tumblers in the safe, which is one of the old variety, refused to operate properly, and the doors could not be opened. Every possible method was used to make the safe open." A blacksmith and a locksmith were called in to help. The paper continued, "If this method doesn't succeed, the safe may be hauled out into the open and … exploded. Should this method prove necessary, it is expected that the movie men will riot for the film rights, and stage a bank-robbing scene on the spot." One hopes that the safe did not contain the money from the Post Office savings accounts.

Back to School or Back to Work?

"The city school authorities are going after parents whose children are engaged in the walnut harvest. … So long as the children and their families have moved out of the city, they cannot be reached by the city school authorities, not being residents in the school district." The Santa Barbara School District planned to bring in truant officers from the state to go after parents in the unincorporated areas of Santa Barbara County.

Under California's 1913 child labor law, a kid as young as 12 was allowed to work if he or she had "completed the prescribed grammar school course and is physically fitted for the work contemplated." Kids were limited to working eight hours a day, up to 48 hours a week! "Street trades," which I suppose meant newsboys, were exempt from this ruling. (My, how things have changed since then!)

Kids in school were also put to work. "The high school manual training department is to save the school board some more hundreds of dollars." How? The Santa Barbara High School's boys' shop classes were constructing playground swings, teeter totters, etc. for elementary school playgrounds.

What About the Power of Prayer?

No one seemed to consider prayer as a means of opening the Post Office safe (but I'm guessing if your money was in it, you would be praying that they would not blow it up.) Anyway, later in September, all the local churches in Santa Barbara were planning "an entire day devoted to prayers for peace [in Europe] and for the success of the 'dry' campaign."

This gentleman is clearly in the "wets" camp.
Image: Library of Congress

There were more and more articles in the 1914 papers about 'drys' (people in favor of prohibiting alcohol) versus the 'wets' (people opposed to prohibiting alcohol). On November 3, 1914, Californians would vote on Proposition Two whose goal was "to prohibit the manufacture, sale, gift or transportation of intoxicating liquors."

Maniacs to Meet at Annual Picnic

Maniacs is another name for persons from Maine. "The Maine Society of Santa Barbara invites all the Maine people in the city to its annual basket picnic in Oak Park Saturday." There must have been a sizeable population of residents from the Pine Tree State in order to host their own picnic. I wonder how many residents of Santa Barbara in 2014 are from the state whose official state beverage is Moxie, an early carbonated beverage.

An Edhatter who is a former resident of Maine had a few words to say about Moxie: Moxie is definitely an acquired taste (I haven't acquired it). It's carbonated and quite astringent. Yes, it is where the term 'she's got lots of moxie' comes from - meaning lots of spunk.

Moxie soft drink is not for the faint of palate.
Image: courtesy of *drinkmoxie.com*

Beating the Heat in 1914

Doesn't it always seem like we get socked with a heat wave right after the school year begins? And so it was on September 18, 1914. "Yesterday was much warmer than any day in the last several weeks, and today Santa Barbarans have been wearing their light summer apparel. White trousers, shirtwaists, and the faithful straw hat have once more come into their own. Soda fountains did a brisk business, and ice cream was in demand."

One place where Santa Barbarans might have gone in 1914 for a refreshing glass of sarsaparilla or a chocolate phosphate was the Gutierrez Drug Store (Phone 62) on the corner of State and Ortega streets (635 State Street). "Established 1855. The Oldest Drug Store in Southern California," according to its ad. The store stayed in business until 1979, although the drugstore was located at various locations in Santa Barbara, and had a succession of owners during its 124 years in business here. How many other local businesses have lasted that long?

Here's a rare photo of the Gutierrez Drug Store in its temporary location on Chapala Street after the 1925 quake. (This probably explains the disorder on the porch.)

Image: courtesy of John Fritsche

The business' founder, Chilean-born Benigno Gutierrez, was a 49er. It is estimated that during the Gold Rush, more than 6,000 men left Chile to go to San Francisco to collect, "Gold, much gold, gold in abundance!" The first version of the Gutierrez Drug Store in 1855 was repurposed from the cabin of a ship that had come aground here. (Recall that until Stearns Wharf was built in 1872, lumber was a scarce commodity in our fair city.)

For most of its existence, the store was in the Fithian Building on State Street. There are some good pix of that building (it's still here!) before and after the quake on pages 78 and 79 of *Santa Barbara, Then and Now* by Neal Graffy.

German Warships in the Channel?

You know people were getting nervous about the war when they thought a German warship was zipping around the Channel Islands. "Believed to have been a German cruiser, presumably the *Leipzig*, a vessel was steaming up the Santa Barbara Channel last night at high speed, with its searchlights coursing the waters. The boat is not thought to be a commercial vessel, as no such craft is possessed of the speed shown, neither would it have been maneuvering its search lights."

Squid boat maybe? Pirates? Panga boat? Paddling around the flotsam and jetsam of the information gyre on the Internet revealed that there was a group of five German cruisers in the Pacific during [spoiler alert! The term "World War" has not been used yet] World War I keeping an eye on Germany's possessions – the Northern Marianas Islands. (Spain sold these islands to Germany in 1899.) Extra Betsy points if you know where these islands are without dipping a toe in the Internet's info gyre.

The SMS Gneisenau *was a sister ship to the* Leipzig *mentioned in the article.*
Image: Wikimedia Commons

The war was affecting people here more and more. "War Means Hard Blow to Seedmen of this County. German Seeds of Many Rich Varieties Cannot Now Be Obtained." Goleta resident Joseph Sexton, Sr. said that our sources for flower and vegetable seeds in Europe would not be available because of "the great war in Europe."

There were several stories in the local press about Santa Barbarans who were stranded in England or Sweden waiting for passage on boats to North America. And two who were not able to escape the German invasion had their cars confiscated. "Two Santa Barbarans Lose Autos in War. ... Two men of prominence, who are Santa Barbarans a considerable part of the year, have had nearly parallel experiences in Germany during the present war. They are George A. Batchelder and William F. Dreer. ...

Both men were twice arrested on suspicion of being spies and both had their motor cars commandeered. This means they were given receipts for their automobiles and at the close of the war, the Germans will be expected to reimburse them." Will they be reimbursed? You will have to read on to find out.

And another fallout from the fighting in Europe – "War is Affecting Most of Musical Instruments Now. Shipments from Germany and France Have Been Stopped by Conflict." However, the problem was seen as opening a door for instrument crafters in the U.S. "According to musical authorities, the war has produced a golden opportunity for the ... manufacture of musical instruments in America." And people in the garment business could also sense a silver lining in the clouds of war judging by this little ditty in the local paper:

"Dressmakers in America,
Find in the war some joy.
For now they know all
*   Paris gowns,*
Must come from Illinois."

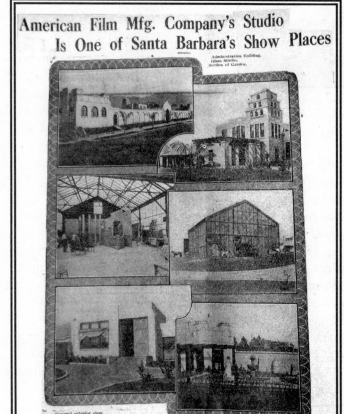

American Film Mfg. Company's Studio Is One of Santa Barbara's Show Places

The American Film Manufacturing Company (aka Flying "A") produced more than 100 movies in 1914.

Image: *Morning Press,* September 13, 1914

The 1915 Cadillac was in the headlines here in September 1914.

Image: courtesy of the New York Public Library

Flying "A" Was Flying High!

Scenes from films were shot in locations such as stores on State Street, the Channel Islands, and all around the county and beyond. Many interior scenes were shot in the company's large glass studio. Pictured here is the headquarters that was located on the corner of Mission and Chapala streets.

A few of the original buildings still remain, most notably the building shown in the top left of the photo.

First Eight-Cylinder Car Coming Next Year!

"There is an air of expectancy and eager anticipation in the Cadillac garage, 136 State Street, where A.L. Smith has charge of the Cadillac business in this territory. This is due to the announcement of the Cadillac Company of their new 1915 car. It is an eight-cylinder car, the first to be put on the American market by an American company." The article went on to say that the first Cadillac had only one cylinder! But the eight-cylinders on the 1915 model were expected to allow the car to soar above its predecessors. "It gives it the highest possible hill-climbing ability … The tests have proven it to have an efficiency on hills which has hitherto been undreamed of." More powerful cars probably allowed the development of hillsides in Santa Barbara such as the Riviera.

Dancing On Her Own Two Feet

She must have been someone that they knew would go far. If Santa Barbara High School had had a "student most likely to succeed" vote in 1913, the year she graduated, she would have been in the running. In addition to being popular, she seemed to be good at so many things – basketball, drama, writing, student council, dancing. "She was a darned good ballroom dancer," a fellow student remembered. In the end, she decided that dancing was the path she would follow.

A small notice in the local paper in October 1914 indicated that she was on her way. "Miss Martha Graham, daughter of Mrs. G.G. Graham of 1323 De La Vina Street, left for Los Angeles today where she will become a student at the Cumnock School of Expression." We know now that her career would span seven decades and take her to audiences around the world. Had she thought or dreamed that big?

From then on, everything happened quickly. She studied dance and movement, and by 1919, she was teaching dance in Los Angeles.

Her life was a series of firsts: the first dancer to perform at the White House, the founder of the first American dance company, and the first dancer to receive the Presidential Medal of Freedom. Her influence and fame linger still.

To celebrate what would have been her 117th birthday on May 11, 2011, Graham became Google's logo for a day.

Martha and her family occupied the home at 1323 De La Vina Street. It belongs to the Upham Hotel and has been converted into their "Country House" consisting of eight guest rooms

One Edhat reader studied under Martha: "Martha Graham was my dance instructor in NY! She was a serious, stern teacher and shaped a strong dance foundation to this day! She would draw attention to each individual student (by gently tapping ankles with a long ruler) to correct proper turn out position until the student had it perfected to meet her standards!"

Left: Graham was considered unusual because she danced barefoot.
Image: courtesy Library of Congress

Center: Graham is clearly expressing joy at being a Google icon for a day.
Image: courtesy of Google

The home that was rented by the Graham family is still with us.
Image: Betsy J. Green

The Wandering Cow and the Traveling Dog

Okay, I'll start with the cow. "Cow Views State Street by Night," read the headline. It must have been a slow news day, because the local paper devoted five! paragraphs to the "cowscapade," which sounds like a great idea for a silent movie scenario. (Actually, that would be a great title for a movie.) "A cow who got it into her head she wanted to see what State Street looked like … managed to see a few things before … interested citizens took the bovine in charge and tied her back on Cota Street." The cow had wandered up and down the sidewalk on State Street startling people in restaurants and pool rooms before she was returned to her home. (Back in the "Old Spanish Days," wandering cows on the streets of our fair city were not news, but that was then, and this was 1914.)

"Canine Caper!" (How's that for another movie idea? I'm just full of ideas today. I'm full of other stuff as well, according to some of my "friends.") Anyway, another four-legged figure on State Street in October was a small dog nicknamed Speedy who wanted to ride on the streetcar. "The conductor put her off … but Speedy wasn't discouraged, and when the car stopped to let off a passenger, … on she jumped, only to be again put off. This happened several times, until finally a passenger, who had watched the determination of the little animal, paid her fare, and Speedy had the much coveted ride." (I always say, it pays to be persistent.)

Vivian Rich was a popular leading lady at the Flying "A" studio.

Image: courtesy of the Library of Congress

More Dogs in the News

Another dog story appeared this month, this time in the *Motion Picture News* magazine in its October 17, 1914 issue. (Thanks to SB film archivist Tonia Guerrero for tossing it my way. Bark! Bark!) Two Santa Barbara youngsters, Effie and Georgia Johns, gave a collie to Vivian Rich, one of the leading ladies of the Flying "A" Film Company here. Vivian, who clearly had a sense of humor, in addition to her good looks, named the dog "Guess."

"Miss Rich takes keen delight in being asked the name of her new pet," wrote the fanzine. "Without a smile, she will say, 'Guess,' and of course the inquirer calls to mind every conceivable name. Not being successful, the usual inquiry is, 'Well, what do you call him?'" And so the game continues.

To Your Health!

In November 1914, California voters would go to the polls to give a thumbs-up to prohibiting alcohol or a bottoms-up for continuing to imbibe. Not surprisingly, companies that sold or manufactured alcohol were starting to get the shakes. In October 1914, an ad in the local paper for Duffy's Pure Malt Whiskey claimed that its product had medicinal benefits.

**"Taken as directed, you avoid and relieve distressing stomach disorders. Get Duffy's and keep well. …
Write for medical booklet."**

So now you know! To your health! Let's keep those Irish eyes smiling.

The Ride of His Life – Almost!

The headline read, "Wild Sea Gives Thrills to Trip of Injured Man," so of course, I have to include this one. The week that began on Monday, October 19, 1914 was not a good one for 55-year-old Arthur Joshua (A.J.) Caire, the man whose father owned Santa Cruz Island, one of the Channel Islands. First, he had a serious riding accident on the island when, "a spirited horse he was trying to ride whirled and threw him to the ground." Caire's leg was broken. The island's residents used planks from wooden boxes to make splints for his leg. Fortunately, his doctor in Santa Barbara made house calls (remember house calls?), and bravely "made a night journey in a little launch across the stormy channel to the island Monday night, arriving … after 11 o'clock at night."

The next day, the doctor and Caire sailed to Santa Barbara in the large yacht belonging to the Santa Cruz Island Company. The sea was still extremely rough, and it must have been an unpleasant voyage for Caire. In fact, it was so rough, that when the yacht arrived about 5:00 p.m., it could not tie up to Stearns Wharf. The doctor and two of the crewmen rowed to the wharf where an ambulance and stretcher were waiting. They returned to a yacht on a motorboat with the stretcher. The injured man was put onto the stretcher, lowered down to the boat, and taken to the wharf.

"Nearly 50 spectators were gathered there," wrote the paper. "Here the most exciting part of the journey occurred, and resembled parts of the sea scenes in Jack London's *Sea Wolf*. The heavy seas, dashing against the wharf, made it impossible to keep the launch steady. It heaved high in the air with each swell, and several times,

the boat crew was nearly dashed overboard. Finally, in a moment when the sea was comparatively calm, three men jumped for the landing, each hanging on to the stretcher on which Mr. Caire lay. The boat on its backward heave swung out three feet from the wharf, and only by desperate exertions did the men keep the island owner from tumbling into the sea. Mr. Caire himself seized a rope and held on to the landing with both hands, to help his men." Whew! No doubt some prayers and bad words were thrown to the winds, but the patient was finally transported safely to Saint Francis Hospital. He eventually recovered from his injury.

Unfortunately, there were no photos of this exciting episode. Caire was an amateur photographer, but obviously was not in a position to take a "selfie" under such extreme circumstances.

A.J. Caire examines a photo outside his photo studio.
Image: courtesy of the Santa Cruz Island Foundation

A 100-year-old electric car looking pretty good for its age.
Image: Dana Newquist

What Goes Around Comes Around – Electric Cars in 1914

An ad in the local paper for electric cars caught my eye. I contacted Dana Newquist, classic car collector, to see if he knew anyone in Santa Barbara with a vintage electric car. No luck! Dana said old-time electric cars are extremely rare.

These cars were popular with women because the engine did not have to be hand cranked. Dana added that women began to drive combustion-engine cars when electric starters came on the scene. And just when I despaired of finding a 1914 electric car, Dana came through for me with a photo of a dandy 1914 Rauch & Lang that he saw at a recent vintage car show. Thank you, Dana! What a cutie! (The car, that is.)

According to the National Museum of American History's website, the Rauch and Lang Carriage Company manufactured these vehicles in Cleveland, Ohio. The company's ad for this car said that it was "the one best adapted for driving by women and children." Cars for kids? Really?

Another reason why women may have been reluctant to drive automobiles was the high rate of breakdowns. An item in the local paper mentioned that a chauffeur for the Flying "A" Film Company had just returned to Santa Barbara after a road trip to San Diego and back. The article casually mentioned that nothing serious had happened on the trip – they only had four flat tires! Yowza! I guess this was routine in times when tires were flimsier, roads were rougher, and men were men ....

A 1914 electric car appeared in the Flying "A" production *A Modern Rip Van Winkle* shot this month. The movie follows a fictional man who has been in prison for 25 years (since 1889) and discovers that the world of 1914 is light years ahead of the world he remembers.

One of the scenes in the movie was filmed at the Hope Ranch Club House. According to the local paper, San Francisco Mayor James Rolph and his wife were extras in this scene. They are seated at the table on the left.

The Hope Ranch Clubhouse, where this was filmed, is now a private home.
Image: courtesy of Neal Graffy

This story inspired one Edhat reader: "Imagine if the astronomical cost and effort that the world - especially America - has spent in the past 100+ years promoting gasoline and internal combustion engines, had instead been put into developing electric vehicles? The world would be a much quieter, healthier place, climate change would not be the pressing issue it is today and pollution/smog would be a fraction of current levels. Oil would not be such a hot commodity, and we would have been spared the ongoing horror of sending our young men and women overseas into danger zones, on the taxpayers' dime, to fight wars in order to enrich the bottom lines and personal bank accounts of privately owned fossil fuel corporations, their executives and stockholders. Can't change history, but it's a nice thought."

Turkey dinner for $1. Of course, the average take-home pay was less than $1,300 per year in 1914.

Image: *Daily News & Independent,* November 24, 1914

100-Year-Old Turkey Dinner

We celebrated Thanksgiving here in November 1914 pretty much the same way that we do today – with a good old-fashioned turkey dinner. Way back when, you could get a turkey dinner with all the trimmings at The Palms restaurant in Carpinteria for one dollar. Today, that same dinner would cost you – oops! Never mind. The restaurant is no longer open on Thanksgiving Day! But The Palms restaurant is still here at 701 Linden Avenue in Carp where it has been since 1912.

Fireless Cookers, the "Modern Kitchen Marvels" of 1914

There were a number of ads 100 years ago for the Ideal Company's Fireless Cook Stove. What is a "fireless cook stove," you ask? It was actually a proto-crockpot that was modeled on a do-it-yourself slow cooker that some women had been using for decades.

"Fireless" is somewhat misleading, but that's advertising for ya. Right? Here's how it worked: (1) Heat some soup or stew in a pot on the stove. (2) Remove the pot from the stove and cover it. (3) Insulate the pot by wrapping a quilt around it, or if you want to be fancy, put the hot pot in a larger pot and pack straw around it. (4) Leave the pot slowing cooking on its own until lunch or supper.

The Ott Hardware Company here gave demonstrations of this "Modern Kitchen Marvel" at its 727 State Street location in October, so apparently this was a new concept for Santa Barbara housewives. Looking like a large cedar chest, the fireless cook stove came in three sizes that could hold one, two, or three pots in its insulated interior. It

Clearly, the concept of slow cookers predates Crock-pots.

Image: *Morning Press,* October 17, 1914

was an addition to a stove, not a replacement. So you needed a sizeable kitchen to have both items.

"Fireless cooking is the most hygienic, the most practical, and the most economical method of cooking ever known, for it saves more than half the kitchen work," according to the ad in the local paper. The Ideal Company claimed, "The Ideal Fireless Cook Stove will save 50 percent of your kitchen labor, 75 percent of your fuel, and add 100 percent to the quality of your food. ... It is not a luxury, but an economy." These devices were popular in the early decades of the 20th century. The popularity of fireless cookers probably cooled as smaller electrical slow cookers were introduced in the 1930s.

Hoosier cabinets maximized storage and convenience.

Image: *Daily News & Independent,* October 23, 1914

The Must-Have Kitchen Cabinets from the Heartland

Of course, kitchens way back when did not have dishwashers, wine coolers, or latte fluffers, but did you know that many kitchens did not even have cabinets? Enter – ta da! – the Hoosier cabinet! Pronounced WHO-zher, these cabinets were usually made of wood, with storage space above and below, and a metal working surface in the middle. Above, there was space for dishes, a spice rack, hooks for egg beaters, rolling pins, spatulas, etc. Many cabinets included a flour sifter. The lower part had shelves for pots and pans. Every square inch was utilized.

The cabinets began to be manufactured around the turn of the century by several companies in Indiana, hence the name. They were quite popular in the early decades of the 20th century. As factories began to focus on efficiency in the workplace, early domestic scientists – usually women – turned their attention to making kitchens more efficient for housewives.

The ads in the Santa Barbara papers stressed the health benefits of Hoosier cabinets. "Your own physician will tell you that too much drudgery in the kitchen is responsible for many of women's serious nervous troubles. You can't take the rest he recommends so long as you walk miles every day in the kitchen preparing and clearing after meals. But you can save this injurious and unnecessary walking with the wonderful new Hoosier Cabinet. ... Every woman who has seen it, is enthusiastic."

There is a Hoosier Cabinet Museum in Nappanee, Indiana. (Well, what else does Nappanee have to put in a museum?) According to the museum's website, as many as 40 companies made Hoosier Cabinets. The website notes that these cabinets faded in popularity in the 1930s and 1940s when new homes began to have built-in cabinets.

Good Taste Never Goes Out of Style (Pun Intended!)

Crockpots saw a resurgence in 1971 when the Rival Company introduced the Crock-Pot (with a hyphen) which sat on kitchen counters next to the harvest-gold electric fondue pot and the avocado-green electric popcorn popper. One website says that today more than 80 percent of American households have a slow cooker. I suspect they are more common in areas that have real winter.

Well, I say it's about time for fondue pots to make a comeback, dontcha think? However, I do hope avocado-green appliances *never* come back. What *were* we thinking?

Here's just one of the six images that make up Edmondson's panorama.

Image: courtesy of the Library of Congress

Notice in the photo that the "tail light" is clearly an afterthought.

Image: courtesy of the Library of Congress

Many thanks to Neal Graffy who was able to pinpoint the location of the photo. The large white house, closest to the camera, still exists at 601-603 West Ortega Street, on the corner of San Pascual Street.

A 10-Foot-Long Photo of Santa Barbara

Articles in the local papers in October and November 1914 discussed the work of photographer A.R. (Alfred Robert) Edmondson who had "a special camera with special lenses ... With it he will be able to get a 10-foot picture. ... For the last several months, Mr. Edmondson has been traveling over every part of the county taking the views, and the results of his labors are now in photographic form at his studio. The book will soon be issued."

Alas, either Edmondson never finished his project or copies no longer exist, because an exhaustive computer search and checking with local collectors only turned up one photo. But it is a wowzer! In fact, it's one of the best – and perhaps, the largest – photo of Santa Barbara. A.R. stood on the eastern edge of the Mesa with his special camera and captured a stunningly clear image of Santa Barbara in 1914.

Watch Your Back!

Cars were becoming more commonplace on Santa Barbara streets, but there were some advantages to horse-powered vehicles. Horses had, well, horse sense. Now that people were driving "horseless carriages," more safeguards were needed to keep people, and horses, safe. The Santa Barbara City Council met in November 1914 and decided that all vehicles must have "conspicuous tail lights." Although there was "strenuous opposition" to the amendment, the councilmen kicked it in the rear and passed the regulation.

Image: Library of Congress

More German Ships in the Channel

In September 1914, some people thought they saw a German warship in the Channel. Now, in November, one Santa Barbara ship captain saw one – up close and personal. "Stopped by Warboat," read the headline. "Ira Eaton, of the launch *Sea Wolf*, is said to have been stopped by a German cruiser, while going from Santa Cruz Island to San Pedro. He says the warboat bought from him 900 pounds of smelt at a good price." Eaton reported the transaction to the authorities in San Pedro.

War News

Hands Across the Atlantic

The good folks in Santa Barbara were finally sitting up and taking notice of the war in Europe. And they were beginning to take action as well. There were several fundraisers in November 1914. One of the most notable was at the home of Stewart Edward White. White was an author, adventurer, and big game hunter. (Animal lovers should skip the next paragraph.)

"Stewart Edward White's museum of trophies is to be opened to the public … [these were not bowling trophies, dear readers, the trophies were animal heads stuck on plaques] for the benefit of the unfortunate Belgians. … [his personal museum] contains 71 different specimens of big game including 65 different species from all parts of the sporting world. … In this museum also will be seen the rifles used on the African trip, and also older weapons formerly used in this country."

(Okay, animal lovers can start reading again.) Apart from looking at dead stuff that was stuffed, participants were also treated to a dance performance by actors from the Flying "A" movie studio. One youngster did a "rag" dance to ragtime music which was popular in 1914. Scott Joplin, of course, was the king of ragtime.

"Her head up, her tail thrashing from side to side, her ears laid back, she stood there looking the landscape over carefully point by point. She was searching for us, but as yet could not locate us. It was really magnificent."

From the book African Camp Fires *by Stewart Edward White, 1913*

Women "Do Their Bit"

The event at the museum raised $1,400, but money was not the only thing that the Whites donated to the war effort. Mrs. Stewart Edward White (Elizabeth) headed the Belgian Relief Fund here and organized a group of local women in "sewing, bandage-making, and knitting." For women who were not handy with a needle, the group had four bandage-rolling machines.

Swords into Plowshares?

Well, sometimes my research leads me in unexpected directions. While looking for a World War I image showing women's contributions, I came across a colorful poster illustrating all the hospital-related items that women made.

Sharp-eyed readers may notice that the item on the upper right is identified as a "tampon." A quick patrol around the Internet revealed that these items were used to stop the bleeding from bullet wounds during World War I, and only after the war, did tampons begin to be manufactured for women.

So now you know. Period.

Women sewed, knitted, and rolled bandages for the war effort.

Image: courtesy of the Library of Congress

Santa Barbara Transfer Co. Has Splendid New Building

New Fireproof Warehouse with Electric Burglar Alarm on Southern Pacific R.R. Spur.

Recognize this building? It's one of the larger buildings in the Funk Zone.

Image: *Morning Press,* November 4, 1914

The Funk Zone Has a History Too, Ya Know

The Funk Zone is often overlooked by people looking at architectural history, so it was cool to find a sketch of a new building in 1914 that is (whoopee!) still here in 2014.

(This building was not included in Neal Graffy's best-selling *Santa Barbara: Then and Now* book, probably because it wasn't pretty enough. Hey, Neal, here's an idea for a Santa Barbara history book that hasn't been done yet – *Ugliest Buildings of Santa Barbara: See Them Now Before They Are Condemned for Crimes Against Architecture*, and how about some simulated action shots of them being imploded? I'm just full of stellar ideas today.)

So anyway, back to the building, which is not really ugly, just warehousey. It sits at 25 East Mason Street, on the corner of Helena Avenue. Today, it's generally known as the former Bekins Moving and Storage Building, which it was for many years. Viewed from above, you can see that the structure is not a rectangular shape because the railroad tracks run along the north side of the building, and the railroad was crucial to its history.

Way back when, wealthy people who lived in places with crappy weather, such as Chicago or Schenectady, would come to Santa Barbara and stay for a whole season. These were the people who used "summer" and "winter" as verbs. Example, "Where do you summer/winter?" (I guess if you practice saying this enough, your friends will stop laughing – eventually.)

Well, dear readers, when you travel this way, you need a big honking trunk to carry all your stuff – think about all those layers of petticoats, corsets, white gloves, etc. Not to mention hats with bird feathers. So people who summered or wintered here would arrive by train with a trunk, or two or three. And people who summer or winter just couldn't schlep their stuff to the Potter Hotel or the Arlington. What would people say?

Hence, the need for "transfer companies." They were not called "moving companies" way back when. The first name for this building was the Santa Barbara Transfer Company. The company helped people move and store their belongings.

This building was recently sold to "an unnamed local investor." The asking price was $21.5 million. Hmmm … Do people with $21.5 million use summer and winter as verbs?

The building sits at the corner of Mason Street and Helena Avenue.

Image: Betsy J. Green

Christmas Gift Ideas in 1914

At the Western Book and Toy Shop at 816 State Street, there were toy soldiers (infantry and battalion) and dolls "from the tiniest kewpie kid to big dollies as large as a three- or four-year-old child. For these dolls, there are kitchen sets, dishes, all kinds of furniture, including pianos, trunks, drums, tops of all kinds, trains of cars, horses and carts, everything in musical and mechanical toys, cattle, lumber and coal cars, a large line of stuffed animals, games of all kinds … a full line of wheel goods, such as hand cars, velocipedes, … dolls' buggies, children's desks, balls, roller skates, … radiopticans."

For mom, gift suggestions ranged from Hoosier cabinets (prices started at $35 and were available on the installment plan), fireless cookers, to electric toasters, to "a box of Phoenix guaranteed hose." For dad, how about a smoking jacket, an electric shaving mug (I guess it was heated?), a leather arm chair, or maybe electric Christmas tree lights?

Some people still used candles on their trees. Years ago, I interviewed an older gentleman who had been a kid during World War I. He told me that at Christmas time, his parents would not let him play at the homes of friends who had electric tree lights. The old lights were hot and were known to start fires because people left them on for too long. Whereas, candles on the tree were lit on Christmas Eve, enjoyed, and extinguished in a matter of minutes.

SECRETS OF THE SEASON

Image: *Daily News & Independent,* December 5, 1914

The increasing hostilities in Europe were affecting the types of presents that children found beneath their trees on Christmas morning in Santa Barbara. Many toys that were normally imported from Europe were not available this year.

Image: Library of Congress

Something New Under the Tree

While many of the Christmas gift ideas in 1914 were old standards, there was something new to place under the tree this year in Santa Barbara – decorative Craftsmen pottery created by Frederick H. and Agnes M. Rhead (pronounced "reed"). The Rheads bought a bungalow on the northwest corner of Foothill and Tornoe roads in the middle of 1913, and converted it into their studio. They built a kiln there in September 1913. (The small wooden building is still there.)

Frederick had been born in England in 1880 to a family that had been creating pottery for generations. It is not surprising that he chose the Foothill-Tornoe location for his studio – Christopher Tornoe (for whom the road is named) was a silversmith. Mission Canyon was a popular spot for other artists as well. The pottery that the Rheads created in their Mission Canyon studio was sold there ("A delightful 10-minutes' walk from the Mission," according to their ad) or downtown at the Nathan Bentz shop at State and Victoria streets.

"With the exception of those forms which obviously must be made

This Rhead vase sold for $150,000 at an auction in 2012.

Image: courtesy of artfixdaily.com

in a mold, … everything is made on the potters' wheel. There is no mechanical method of decoration or duplication of design." Clearly targeting a high-end clientele, the Rheads held a private exhibition of their work at the Bentz shop on December 3. The invitations were described as "artistic little folders." The Rheads stayed here for several more years. In the 1930s, after he had left our fair city, Frederick turned his hand to an equally artistic, but more plebian form of pottery – the colorful Fiesta dinnerware.

His art pottery remains popular with collectors. A Rhead vase sold for $150,000 at a recent auction. (At that price, I'm sure you pronounce it "vahz" and not "vace.") Mission Canyon denizens report finding pottery shards in the area from time to time. Hmmm. I wonder what genuine Rhead shards would bring at auction? They probably make dandy paperweights.

Remember Christmas Savings Accounts?

These have pretty much fallen by the wayside, probably because of credit cards, but ever since 1909 when the first Christmas saving club was started in Pennsylvania, they were popular with millions of Americans. In December 1914, the Santa Barbara Savings and Loan Bank encouraged people to sign up (and pony up) to pay for holiday gifts in 1915. As many as 500 local citizens participated in 1914. You could pay $1 a week or as little as 5¢ which you then increased by 5¢ a week for 50 weeks. The Christmas clubs basically kept you from spending your money. Oh, and the bank offered four percent interest for people who stayed with the plan all year. Four percent interest – those were the days, eh?

Bet You Didn't Know This!

Image: courtesy of the New York Public Library

An ad in the local paper for the Smith Brothers hardware store at 625 State Street selling "weed chains" put my curiosity in gear. "Don't run the risk of an accident during muddy weather," read the ad. "One skid may cost you more than several sets of chains." What the heck were weed chains? Sounds like tire chains for snow. Were they made out of hemp?

A few googles later, I learned all about weed chains – and also their connection to Harry Houdini! Weed chains were invented by Harry Delyne Weed of Syracuse, New York, a city that gets 66 inches of snow a year. While tire chains are used primarily for snow today, way back when in 1914, they were also a good idea in places with dirt roads. (In 1914, 70 out of the 80 miles of roads in Santa Barbara were dirt or mud, depending on the season.)

And the connection to Houdini? One of his most famous acts took place for the first time in 1908 when he was wrapped in six sets of tire chains. The chains were none other than – Weed tire chains! After 30 minutes, Houdini was able to free himself. Houdini made the national news – and so did Weed chains. I never tire of history. (Pun intended!)

The King of Comedy Conquers Santa Barbara

1914 marked the American debut of 25-year-old Charlie Chaplin. He appeared in more than 30 movies – most of them quite short – in 1914, but by December, he had 'em rolling in the aisles in local theaters. "Charles Chaplin is Keystone Comedian," read the headline. "Today will be the last day the Santa Barbara public will have to see the popular Keystone comedy, *Tillie's Punctured Romance,* a six-reeler (1 hour, 20 minutes) that also starred Marie Dressler. The paper continued, "Without question, this has proven the most popular photoplay ever shown in Santa Barbara. Capacity houses have enjoyed every performance."

Chaplin appeared in more than 80 movies, but were any of them filmed in Santa Barbara? I asked this question of Dana Driskel, studio professor of Film & Media Studies at UCSB. His answer – in a word, "no." "Mutual, Flying A's distributor, signed Chaplin to a major contract and I'm sure the idea was floated to have him produce his films in SB on the Flying A lot – the biggest and newest one on the coast in early 1916 – but he negotiated for his own studio, Lone Star, (note the name) and built the studio in Hollywood. He very likely participated in real estate deals here and there but so did almost every major star with money to invest." So, although Washington never slept here, Chaplin may have.

Image: courtesy of the Library of Congress

Gather 'Round the Christmas Tree

Many Santa Barbarans think that the Norfolk Island Pine at the northwest corner of Carrillo and Chapala streets has always been the "official Christmas tree," but there have been other trees so designated. In 1914, there was a move to collect money to cut down a tree in the Santa Ynez Mountains and haul it into Santa Barbara, but perhaps for economic reasons, a living tree was chosen. The tree was described as a 40-foot-tall Cypress tree at the southwest corner of the courthouse property at Anacapa and Figueroa streets. There are a couple of trees near that corner today, but none is a Cypress. Perhaps the newspaper got the name wrong, or perhaps the tree was replaced by another over the years.

Santa Barbara historian Hattie Beresford told me that the Norfolk Island Pine at Chapala and Carrillo streets that we now decorate has been the Community Christmas tree since 1928, although there were a few years when another tree was substituted. The Chapala-Carrillo tree was planted in 1877 when there was still an adobe house on that corner.

A tree near the old courthouse was the city's Christmas tree in 1914 (seen in this 1923 photo).

Image: courtesy of the Santa Barbara Historical Museum

Over the years, the tree has continued to survive while the neighborhood around it has changed from an adobe to the YMCA to a vacant lot and now Ralphs Grocery Store.

Now here's something I didn't know when I started writing this story. I am a stickler for punctuation and I always assumed that Ralph's should be written with an apostrophe between the h and the s. But no, dear readers, I was mistaken! It should be apostropheless, or perhaps Ralphs' with an apostrophe at the end. The grocery story was founded by George Albert Ralphs, who opened his store in Los Angeles in 1873. (Aren't you glad that I have the time to research such minutiae so that you don't have to?)

Dress Code, Chaperones, and Zero-Tolerance for Chewing Gum

Well, the tango may have been tolerated at the local hotels, but there would be no dirty dancing allowed at Santa Barbara High School's first dance in the newly built Recreation Center at the corner of Carrillo and Anacapa streets. Also banned for the evening were bright socks and loud neckties on boys. Spooning and joyrides were nixed as well. "A chaperone must accompany every vehicle occupied by high school students which leaves the dance hall." And leave the chewing gum at home (or at least, park it behind your ear.)

A dance too hot to handle!

Image: courtesy of the New York Public Library

Was It or Wasn't it?

"Meteor Falls in Mission Canyon," according to the headline in the local paper. "Entire Northern Sky Illuminated for Several Seconds." The meteor described as "a ball of fire that was bright even in the moonlight, is believed to have fallen in upper Mission Canyon. The aerial visitor made its appearance about 7:00 last evening and was seen and heard by several persons in the vicinity of the Old Mission. … The meteor first made its appearance above Cold Springs … The meteor was in plain sight about four seconds and as it fell, there was a swishing sound … The ball of fire was about a quarter the size of the full moon, and as it disappeared, its entire course was a trail of sparks."

People in Goleta also reported seeing the fiery object hurtling through the air. Heavens to Betsy!

Image: NASA

The Pasadena Tournament of Roses began in 1890.
Image: courtesy of the New York Public Library

Everything's Coming Up Roses!

The call went out on December 19 for roses for our city's float in Pasadena's Tournament of Roses. The Santa Barbara Chamber of Commerce issued a request for "the best pink and white flowers Santa Barbara can produce. … The tentative plan for Santa Barbara's float is to feature Saint Barbara with a girl resembling as nearly as possible the classic picture of Saint Barbara." There were high hopes that we would win the $500 prize for the best municipal float.

By December 23, the idea for a Saint Barbara float morphed into a car decorated as a giant basket of roses. (Sorry, Babs!) As the days passed, the request was ramped up to "an urgent appeal" with float committee members telephoning residents. The situation was beginning to get almost ugly as committee members patrolled the streets and knocked on doors asking for flowers from promising-looking gardens. The paper listed the names of prominent citizens who had contributed flowers. Ahem! Woe betide those whose names were not mentioned!

By December 31, the paper reported that between 5,000 and 6,000 Santa Barbara blooms were shipped to Pasadena to decorate our float.

Continued next year!

Index

Look for **Way Back When: Santa Barbara in 1915**

in bookstores next year.
(Second in the series of Santa Barbara history –
one year at a time.)